WHAT YOUR HANDWRITING REVEALS

WHAT YOUR HANDWRITING REVEALS

How to Master the Art of Graphology

by

Margaret Gullan-Whur

AVENEL BOOKS
New York

This 1986 edition is published by Avenel Books, distributed by Crown
Publishers, Inc., 225 Park Avenue South, New York, New York 10003,
by arrangement with Thorson's Publishing Group, Ltd.

Printed and Bound in the United States of America

LIBRARY OF CONGRESS CATALOGING IN PUBLICATION DATA

Gullan-Whur, Margaret.
  What your handwriting reveals.

  Reprint. Originally published: Wellingborough,
Northamptonshire : Aquarian Press, 1984.
  Includes index.
  1. Graphology. I. Title.
BF891.G85   1986   155.2'82   86-28716

ISBN: 0-517-63236-5

h g f e d c b a

Contents

Acknowledgments

I am very grateful to the following people for their painstaking interest and valuable suggestions:
Dr Dennis Morgan, B.A., M.B., B.Chir., M.R.C.P., D.P.M., D.R.C.O.G., F.R.C.Psych. (Consultant Psychiatrist, West Norfolk and Wisbech Health Authority.)
The Revd. Stephen Cox, B.A. (Marriage Guidance Counsellor. Presently University Chaplain to Surrey University, formerly Norwich Diocesan Youth Chaplain.)
Anne and Bill Armitage,
And my husband Jeremy.
My thanks also go to the British Museum for permission to reproduce their manuscripts,
And to all those who have allowed me to use samples of their writing, helped me with research, or encouraged me to write down my findings.

Introduction

The handwriting of a relative or friend is instantly recognizable. It is a visible witness to its creator's individuality, yet it is normally regarded as a means to an end, rather than as a subject of intense interest in itself. The brain alone provides the impulses which move the pen in the hand, and in the interpretation of these impulses lies the basis of graphology.

The Oxford Dictionary grapples with the subject and finally calls it an 'art or science'. Before making any judgement or further definition I ask you to observe graphology in practice.

Come and sit by me

(A)

Come and sit by me

(B)

To encounter handwriting is to encounter a personality, and as we react instinctively to the human form or voice, so do we react to writing. Choose one of the samples above, and I will tell you about the person beside you.

(A) will be delighted to see you and will do all he can to make you feel welcome. He is an affectionate person who fears solitude and he will make himself as attractive as possible — to begin with. He is also curious to know what you are like. But there is strength and confidence here, and if you disappoint this person by not responding positively to his ways, he will soon loose interest. He is honest, and knows well the sources of his own happiness, and this clarity of vision will help him to accept or reject you before an hour has passed.

(B) is going to show you something interesting, and by the end of an hour will probably know very little about you. You will certainly know very little about him, but may have learned a good deal about Otto the Great or snakes. He is self-disciplined and has marked powers of concentration: to him personal encounters are of less interest than facts.

Both (A) and (B) have told us many other things about themselves in their written invitations. (A) may be outgoing but he is not rash or impulsive, for the dragging of his pen before each word shows much deliberation whilst writing. Such additional preliminary marks are known as cautionary strokes:

_me _sit

(B)'s writing has no such strokes, which does not mean that he acts rashly, but that he tends to think out a plan of action privately before embarking on a project. He will seldom openly dither, so will seem decisive. (A) tells us in his sweeping underloop that he is in harmony with his physical nature and knows how to indulge himself, but (B) appears not to derive pleasure from sheer physical indulgence so much as from working energetically for a cause, or for others.

These and several other characteristics make themselves clear to me from the brief samples above, and longer extracts would bring forth many more traits. I have shown what graphology does but I have not explained how it does it; and because I regard it as a practical help in day-to-day living rather than as a form of esoteric enlightenment entrusted only to the few, I am making this a reference handbook. It should be possible for anyone who so wishes to study and to practise graphology.

Naturally some time must pass before a reader new to the subject can hope to assess a character accurately, but since I believe this is what people want to do, or so I am told by the many groups to whom I give talks, I should like to suggest ways of making a start. Firstly, please read First Impressions without attempting to memorize it. When you have finished it your mind should be attuned to the subject and you will realize that no analysis can be made without constant checking for confirmation. There should be four or five similar strokes in any sample for positive analysis:

this need is emphasized throughout the book, and I have suggested as many cross-references as I can to avoid hasty judgement.

Chapter II contains several hundred different letter formations. Do not assume that the one you seek is not explained because it is not drawn in exactly the same way. Letter forms are dictated by flow and emphasis, and it may be necessary to refer at once to the chapter on Emphasis. Because the reader will naturally want to begin random analysis as soon as possible, may I warn now against using material written specially for the purpose, as its flow may be stylized or stilted. There is seldom any possibility of analyzing accurately the writing of a child under twelve years old, but the immense value of graphology to anyone in contact with young people over that age will be appreciated after reading Understanding Teenagers in Chapter V.

An experienced graphologist must position himself behind the pen and follow the movements of the brain. As in driving a car this semi-automatic response is a possibility for almost anyone, but it does not happen suddenly. Please be prepared to learn slowly, make mistakes and be confused at first: be prepared, too, for your analyses to be taken seriously. A responsible attitude is essential, and if constant reference is made to the first three chapters of this beginner's manual you will eventually find yourself mastering an undoubted force for good.

If you have doubts about the basic principles of graphology, try this experiment. Doodle whilst day-dreaming about an intense physical pleasure, and see the downward plunging of your scribble. Doodle again, applying your brain to a logical or practical problem, and watch the marks move in an even stream across the page. Then raise your thoughts to the plane of philosophy or religion, apply moral or spiritual vision and finally observe what you have drawn: it will probably resemble a range of mountain peaks.

This experiment bears directly on the scope of Chapter III, but it has an introductory function thus: just as a blush produced by thought proves the power of mind over body, so the pattern of a scribble shows mental control in a pen-stroke.

I
First Impressions

1. Slope

When we meet someone for the first time we are usually struck by one or more outstanding attributes of his personality. So it is with writing. When we encountered (A) and (B) it was obvious that there were immediate and marked differences in the slope, flow and spacing of their written words, and these constitute graphological first impressions.

The slope of the writing is concerned with sociability. A strong forward or backward slope indicates an awareness of other people, and a propensity towards influencing or being influenced by them.

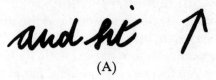

(A)

(A)'s forward sloping hand shows that he reaches out towards people.

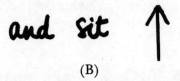

(B)

(B)'s writing is generally upright. Lack of slope (vertical uprights) is found in the writing of those who walk alone, and whose main motivations in life are factors other than their fellow men. (B)'s invitation to sit beside him was given so that you might encounter something specific apart from himself: he did not mind unduly whether you came or not, and was not particularly interested in you. The slope of his writing tells only that he is of an independent nature, though the slight unevenness of the uprights is significant and will be discussed shortly.

We must be quite sure about the angles of the uprights in any handwriting sample. I always hold a pencil against several before making a judgement, since a forward or backward slope can appear very much greater than it is, and apparently upright writing may not be so at all.

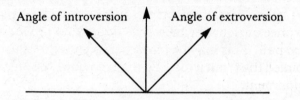

Angle of introversion   Angle of extroversion

(A)'s writing stands at an angle of 45°. This is a strong forward slope but not an excessive one. The example below demonstrates the super-salesman's stream, which is an onward-driving flow set to sweep all obstacles from its path.

The extreme forward angle shows self-projection on to others; the strong letter-linking a lack of caution, and the upward line-slope a thorough conviction in, and enjoyment of what he is doing. The whole picture combines to show a personality who genuinely feels that he is coercing you for your own benefit. Employers of salesmen will look for such a combination: most other employers, beware!

But there is also an introverted super-salesman, and we can use his writing for the study of back-slope:

All writing which slopes backwards, however slightly, shows a pulling away from people. The reasons will vary, and clues to them will be found in other aspects of the writing. Some people use a back-slope at certain times, and they alone will know why they find it necessary to hold others at arm's length when involved in that one sphere of activity.

The salesman above feels compelled to sell you his goods or ideas, not because he is convinced they are excellent and will improve your life, but because if he cannot he feels himself to be a failure. His writing pulls sharply away from people because he either fears or distrusts them. Perhaps he has been deceived in the past or perhaps he was forced unwillingly into a family business. What the graphologist will want to know is whether a backward slope has always been the natural flow of his writing, for handwriting which was once upright or which once sloped forward may develop a backward pull. This may be temporary, caused by hurt feelings or disappointed trust, but it may also happen slowly during a lifetime of disillusionment.

People whose writing shows a random slope are suffering from emotional disturbance.

In (B)'s case the variation is slight:

sit by

This suggests an emotional blow. If the random slope is long-standing it would suggest hurtful parental behaviour in early childhood, and this would certainly tie in with other factors in the writing. The reader may like to examine (B)'s writing again when he has reached the end of Chapter I, and I am sure he will note the obvious links. If, however, the unevenness is newly present, then (B) has suffered a recent emotional injury.

Wildly random uprights indicate severe emotional disturbance. In such instances kindly and tolerant behaviour by others, together with genuine praise and acknowledgement of the writer's talents, will bring about an increase in self-knowledge and self-respect. This will gradually come to show in the writing, and the uprights will have a more regular appearance:

perpendicular style

perpendicular style

Emotional disturbance.

Improved social attitudes.

Mental breakdowns are often preceeded by minor emotional disturbance, and many of the unhappy episodes of adolescence have their roots in poor emotional relationships. I have introduced this important example of the help given by graphology very early in my book for two reasons. Firstly, it is one of the few aspects of analysis which can safely be studied in isolation, and secondly, I mention it in the hope that an awareness of emotional disturbance will show how graphology can help to keep ourselves and others away from the psychiatrist's consulting room.

Remember, uneven uprights indicate emotional disturbance, unhappiness over personal relationships, and possibly unstable emotional reactions.

perpendicular style
Most people

Always check, asking the writer if necessary, whether the diversity is recent, occasionally present, or of long standing. Remember, too, that emotional disturbance is not in itself a mental disorder. For mental disturbance to be present there must always be some distortion of the actual letter formation, and this will be discussed later, in Decoration and Distortion.

2. Line Slope
Although extreme unevenness will be apparent on lined paper, it is obvious that a sample on plain paper is preferable for assessing line slope. An addressed envelope is ideal, and it is often possible to guess the mood of the letter inside by this means.

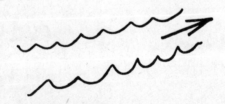

Writing which rises to the right, as above, shows current cheerfulness: a prospective employer might well have faith in the first super-salesman's optimism, for his writing rises gently in this way. Rising signatures are more complex and will be discussed later.

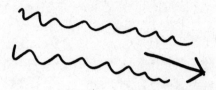

Lines which sag downhill show depression or physical weariness. The development of a negative slope may be the first visible symptom of such a state and can prove valuable. I often quote the occasion when I discovered how exhausted I was by glimpsing a self-addressed envelope on the door mat! (Note especially a falling signature.) Line slope fluctuates considerably and is often no more than a barometer of the mood of the moment. One happy experience is enough to make the lines rise for a day or two, whilst temporary tiredness or disappointment will cause them to droop for a while.

Although frequent slope-changes must indicate a character who is easily elated or downcast, such variation has not the same meaning as a constant rise and fall of the line slope within one piece of writing. Occasional or regular patterns which develop in this way are of special interest. Emotional involvement with the subject matter shows as below:

When I have finished I shall be able to go out whenever I like.

Word size will be uneven as explained on page 36. This pattern reflects uneven heartbeats or excited gasps of breath, but may indicate fury or anxiety as well as passionate love. It is not connected with emotional disturbance unless uneven uprights are also present.

Certain kinds of physical illness may be detected in the line slope, but the sign of tuberculosis once accepted by graphologists is now rare:

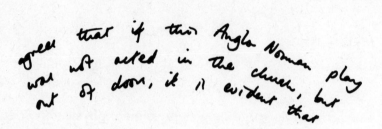

For disruption in the line-slope of signatures see page 170. Before making an assessment of mood, always check that there is not a physical or practical reason for the slope: the writer may have been using a side table, or he may be making a decoration of his script, as in an autograph album.

3. Flow

It could be said that the essence of graphology lies within this heading. Eager outpourings or stilted, suppressed marks reveal alike the state of the mind at their source: the impulsive movements of the pen are controlled by the character who holds it, and every section in this book is but an extension of flow-examination.

The movements of our bodies reflect our inner poise or the lack of it. We all recognize the scurrying gait of the anxious person, the jolly swing which comes from cheerful vitality, the stillness and feeling of controlled power of the sportsman, and the upright dignity of the supremely confident. We are no less impressive in our handwriting, and as we leave it behind as evidence, there is ample time for painstaking analysis. Slope is itself determined by flow. The driving writing of our first aquaintance (A) may not have been written more quickly than (B)'s, but its flow is less restrained. Restraint is shown whenever the pen leaves the paper, and should be interpreted as measured caution unless other factors suggest lack of brain action. Samples of this will be introduced later.

Recent research into electro-encephalographic (brain) patterns suggests that our individual pattern, as well as our temperament and experience, will influence the flow of our writing:

Bach   Yet need I fear no

a certain response

It may vary from the unlinked, or 'painted' note-like writing of the imaginative musician to the heavy super-salesman's stream. Fortunately the days are over when school children were forced to regulate their writing into linked script, italic design, or Victorian copper-plate, and it is at last recognized that a happy flow will produce the tidiest writing.

An unhappy flow induces pronounced variations in stroke size, slope and pressure, and these indicate conflict. People are unconsciously disturbed by such variations when they encounter them, and an employer may take a dislike to an applicant without meeting him.

An awareness of flow should be the first goal of the student graphologist, but since so many factors influence it he should not judge hastily. Brain pattern or aptitudes may dictate it from birth, but experience acting on temperament will modify it. For example, all musicians are not imaginative, or sensitive:

Some are pragmatic or logical (centre case dominated) with tactile skill (tight letter formation and closely dotted *i*.)

Verdi every night

Others are showmen (decorated letters) with a desire to dominate or influence (heavy pressure, with thickening ends to the strokes).

Best Wishes

Others are tactile showmen i.e., virtuosos. (Tight formation, closely dotted *i*, but decorated.)

Such complexities show the need for a systematic approach to the analysis of flow, and *cautionary strokes* are a safe starting-point. They are found in (A)'s writing on page 9, and are a literal dragging of the pen before each word — a visible hesitation or dither. Such writers are not impulsive, and like to peer all round a situation before acting on it. However, once committed they may be hard to stop!

(B)'s writing has no such strokes, which does not mean he acts rashly, but that he tends to think out a plan of action privately before embarking on a project. He seldom hesitates and appears decisive. His lack of cautionary strokes may coincide with a resistance to all joining strokes.

Unlinked script is produced by a particular impulse, and is referred to in my book as 'painted' writing. Here is one example:

thank you very much

The writer of *Bach* was another.

Such writers have in common the attribute of a visual conception of life. Their brain impulses dictate a drawing, rather than a writing of the letter forms, and embody a sense of spacial awareness. The flow of their writing is in harmony with their appreciation of the order around them: they constantly balance and check that things are all moving along consistently. Such people are not necessarily artistic, although this is often the case. They may be gifted at demonstration or presentation work, or simply have a sense of order which their brain commands them to respect, as opposed to loop-makers who are more often emotionally motivated.

Writers who print their letters seldom use cautionary strokes since they do not need brakes to hold back the flow. They have a natural sense of timing. Unfortunately such writers still occasionally find that there is pressure on them from others to link their letters. Self-criticism may add to the coercion of rigid teaching methods or unkind comments, and when this happens the flow becomes distorted, and cautionary strokes are added from anxiety over the physical process of writing:

The brown fox jumps

Sometimes the writer presses the letters together in an effort to make them appear linked:

We practised for ages

Left to write calmly in his own way, such a person will produce well-modulated formations, which will probably have been completed just as quickly as apparently fast-written script:

We practised for ages

Very many people make a break in their writing every four or five letters, regardless of the length of the word. This is called the intuitive or checking pause: the writer stops momentarily to check his progress:

After the dance came the

I liken this to an animal grazing. As long as he lifts his head occasionally to assess that there is no danger around, he is unlikely to be pounced on from behind. Those who make no pauses at all may be rushing blindly into danger or error:

An interesting experience

Sometimes the pause comes before a letter which, because of its stroke direction, is difficult for the writer to link on to:

after the start often

And here the break always follows a certain left-ward turned formation:

symbol, saying your first year

More often, however, the brain appears to dictate a pattern of pauses which bears no apparent relationship to letter forms or manual tiredness, and this pattern should be respected. Writing which is strongly linked shows a preoccupation with one's own thoughts, wishes or will:

An interesting experience

Such an assessment may be modified by pressure and letter endings, but it is easy to feel the intensity of the inner drive in such writing. Cautionary strokes show an awareness of the possibility of rashness, but may not always counter it, and are sometimes no more than a dragging of the pen between words as the mind races on:

An interesting experience

The omission of *t*-strokes and *i* dots in such a hand clearly indicates a character swept along by his own brain waves. Employers beware, but spouses take comfort: your help in double-checking is needed and is probably appreciated.

A racing brain pattern is not necessarily a sign of intelligence, but if the writing is consistently joined on either the upper or lower thinking level, and the letters end lightly or even unintelligibly, then we may assume that a fast-thinking brain lies behind the script.

There are many kinds of intelligence and no one graphological symbol for it: the handwriting of a genius may be marred by emotional disturbance or impatience:

intensely concentrated

whilst the acknowledged world authority on rocks has painted writing and fanatical religious views:

after all my Thought

It is best to assess cerebral qualities in less general terms and on their detailed merits, such as attention to detail, or imaginative logic which is shown by linking on the higher thought levels:

extraordinarily inspired

Retardation of the brain flow is shown by free-standing letters prefaced by a cautionary stroke:

faces

by sluggish, over-formed letters:

The rain falls

by trailing *t*-strokes:

at the time

and by gaps in the centre of letter formations which are not painted ones:

J t. Axelby

(H. Axelby)

Naturally we are referring here to the writing of normally literate people and not to the educationally sub-normal whose writing will be malformed or equivalent to the achievement of their mental age group.

Slowness in writing, as opposed to an alert, bouncing brain pattern which may produce quickly written or painted print, indicates slow thinking. However, there may be gifts apparent to the graphologist which the writer himself imagines he is too dull to possess. The section on Understanding Teenagers provides a helpful checklist.

The flow from the brain may cause the writing to be more strongly linked at one level than at another, as was shown in the sample of imaginatively linked script. Centrally linked writing shows a character who stays in close touch with reality:

she is keen to please

The lower the base of the writing the more practical or earthbound the personality. A current of down-holding can be felt in the writing, forming a pattern like this:

going away ‿‿‿‿‿‿‿‿‿

This aspect of flow is examined in more detail in Chapter III, The Balance of the Personality.

The flow of handwriting is altered by the influence of unnatural agents in the body, such as drink or drugs. There are liable to be signs similar to retardation and absent-mindedness (dragging or absent *t*-strokes) and exhaustion (downward slope). Sometimes the writing will disintegrate as the sample progresses. The suddenness of the change will suggest an unnatural interference with the flow, and this possibility should be considered before attempting to analyze exceptionally careless or disintegrated writing.

Size of handwriting is the least significant of all the aspects of flow, and I am not allowing it a section of its own. After many years · of researching the importance of size I find it to be related to practical considerations as much as to brain impulse. Other graphologists may not agree, but with so many other more reliable facets to analyze, I am not going to give it a prominence which may prove misleading.

The relative size of letters is significant, especially in signatures, but the writing of a balanced person will always try to adapt itself to the space available. Throughout this book the meaning of the word balanced is as follows: a character in which no one impulse of the brain threatens to dominate or overwhelm the whole.

Large writing may show a warm, expansive nature, but it may be used in a gesture which is quite the reverse.

Tommy dislikes writing thank-you letters and wants to fill the page:

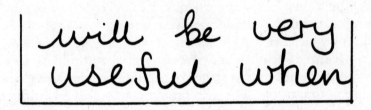

Mrs Parker does not want the milkman to miss her note:

One pint only

Equally pragmatic reasons may lie behind the creation of tiny writing.

Sheila finds notepaper expensive and does not want to waste it:

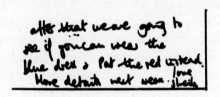

Frank's sense of harmony will not allow him to use his preferred large writing:

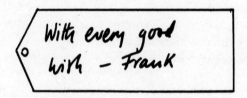

Accordingly, size of writing will only be referred to from now on in relation to other parts of the same writing.

Writing which becomes progressively smaller within one sample, and decreasingly legible, may be connected with illness such as Parkinsonism; but at this stage we should consider size changes in relation to tension. The grip on the pen will clearly influence the appearance of handwriting: manual dexterity will normally result in well-formed and evenly-sized letters, whilst a tired, weak or strained wrist gives a superficially untidy or over-released character to the writing (see page 33).

The enlargement of isolated or individual words has an emotional significance and is discussed on page 36 and in Signatures. The contraction of individual words, often names, through emotional tension, may reduce their size. The size of handwriting can seldom be considered in isolation, though it may corroborate other findings. For example, large writing does not in itself indicate an egotistic nature, but when it includes separated, decorated capitals and other signs of pride and self-projection, it may contribute to that assessment.

4. Spacing

The previous section suggested that separated letters show an awareness of surroundings, and to some extent an ability to adapt to them. Writing with small spaces (two letter widths) between the words shows a character who is willing to allow others to have their say:

when I have finished eating

A balanced space indicates a balanced attitude. Cramped writing belongs to those people who like to be surrounded by others, but are afraid they may be bullied:

when I have finished eating

This is a sociable but defensive position probably resulting from an excess of strong-willed family or schoolmates in childhood.

Wide gaps between words indicate distrust of others or a love of solitude. Although such writing may well show signs of independence such as free-standing *s*'s, wide spacing alone does not prove this, and may be found in lonely, insecure writing. Either way it shows deliberate distancing from others:

When I have finished eating

Wide margins or spaces surrounding blocks of words show visual perception and a sense of order, but only if they are moderate and well-proportioned all round.

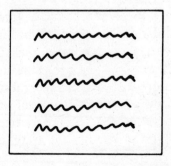

Exaggerated margins at the top or on the left of the paper show reluctance to embark on untried projects:

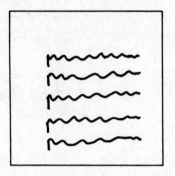

Very wide margins on the bottom or the right show fear of reprisal:

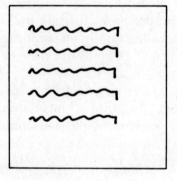

See also leftward signatures on page 167.
    Narrow margins on the top or left show initial confidence:

On the bottom or the right they indicate increasing confidence once the writer has successfully embarked on a project:

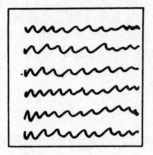

Margins should be examined in letters of application, but in personal correspondence spontaneity is far more important. Lines of writing which encroach upon one another's space are discussed on page 140.

The spaces surrounding signatures are important and are discussed on page 165. No signature should be assessed without the chapter Signatures having first been read and assimilated.

5. Pressure

Suspicions of the supernatural may form in people's minds when they see me run my fingers over the underside of a page of handwriting. In fact, I am simply feeling to discover whether the pressure of the writing has produced grooves and ridges in the page; if it has we are confronting a strong personality, both mentally and physically.

Heavy pressure — impossible to reproduce in print — shows forcefulness and generally good health. The writing may be thick, and its creator will probably choose a wide or thick nib in an instinctive desire for proportion and harmony:

going after lunch

A thin nib or a sharp pencil will cut the paper:

going after lunch

To be certain about the nature of the force we must read the chapter on The Balance of the Personality, for the flow could be channelled in more than one direction, but consistently heavy pressure generally indicates strength in all facets of the personality.

In very sensitive or physically weak writing no pressure will be felt, and the emphasis will at first appear even:

This boy is reasonably good

Light overall pressure shows sensitivity, in itself a lack of strength, but this quality may be misleading. It is always necessary to investigate emphasis (page 48) and balance, (Chapter III).

We have already seen a link between light writing and living in the imagination:

Bach extraordinarily inspired

There is a link between heavy writing and practical or physical pursuits, often in connection with the earth, or animals:

six acres of

In a generally earthbound hand light writing will signify ill-health whilst in an upward-pulled hand heavy pressure indicates repression, self-control or great physical strength. Here are two characters who prove the complex problem that the interpretation of pressure can be:

depends on sales

Heavy pressure with yielding *s*'s indicates a gentle giant (above). But do not be misled by the following sample, for the old lady who wrote it is weak in the knees alone:

visit my sister

Light pressure indicating illness is discussed much later in Diagnosis of Illness. However, general debility or tiredness may cause an overall withdrawal of pressure, and will probably be accompanied by a downward line slope and drooping *t*-strokes:

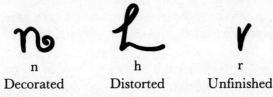

Strong pressure may be masked by thick writing, and small fine writing may belie the pressure behind it: this is why I test the underside of the paper. Uneven pressure within letters is normal and is discussed in the section on Emphasis which follows the Alphabetical Lists. In writing where there is a strong sense of rhythm the graphologist may feel ebb and flow in the pressure.

Writer's Fatigue due to excessive writing
This physical condition will produce lighter, less legible writing as shown in the sample of rough notes on page 33. There will not be any other signs of disturbance unless they are normally present in the writing, though occasionally the effects of lessened control may be interesting. These usually take the form of additional loops, which are explained in Chapter III. 'Writer's Cramp' is a psycho-physical condition. Its early stages are indicated on page 34, and recent medical thinking discussed on page 35 in Distortion.

6. Decoration and Distortion
It is very important to understand the difference between decorations, which are additions to wholly and correctly formed letters, and distortions, which are malformed letters. Letters written hurriedly and not completed are not distorted, but unfinished.

n	h	r
Decorated	Distorted	Unfinished

All three appear so regularly in signatures that analysis of these should not be made on the basis of this section, but after studying the chapter on Signatures. Decorations spring from many impulses of the mind, but they all have one point in common, which is that the writer does not like the look of his writing unless it is embellished. The following three samples are decorated.

Mr Clark thinks that modern life has nothing of the style or charm of former days. He wears a fob watch and would not mind being described as eccentric:

the pleasure of

Robert feels that no one ever notices him. He is unremarkable in appearance and doubts if the headmaster knows his name. He is sixteen:

answer the question

Mrs Simpson sews frills and braid on everything. She thinks her sister's house and clothes are 'plain':

Happy Birthday

Decorations are almost always deliberate, but the writer would be surprised and hurt to hear them described as vanity. Like the wearer of blue hair, a loud tie or a sequinned dress she or he is 'trying to look nice'. Decorations on handwriting should be regarded in the same light, and psychological reasons left to behaviourists.

Distortions are quite different, and the most common are discussed in detail in the alphabetical lists. Unfortunately, however, it is the distorted letter which the newcomer to graphology is most likely to be curious about, and he may be disappointed in the list. Careful reading of the section on Emphasis should help to discover the reason for the distortion, and most will come within the following categories.

Greek letter performing the conscious role of decoration. This formation is not taught in school nowadays, so is a chosen refinement:

$$\varepsilon \quad \epsilon$$

Letter deliberately made easier to write. We must suspect laziness, tiredness or weakness in the lower body. Other factors in the writing will weigh heavily in favour of one particular interpretation. For example, downward sloping lines and drooping *t*-strokes will indicate tiredness:

This flattened *h* has an earthward pull, and shows a childish attitude towards money matters. All downward flattened letters show a reluctance to allow logic or philosophy (the higher parts of the mind which develop after early childhood) to influence decisions. If, however, this is the only such *h* in a large sample, it should be classed as an unfinished letter:

Many distortions are due to an imbalance of the personality, the letter being pushed or pulled upward or downward by a brain impulse as was the *h* above. Other distorted letters are caused by physical handicaps.

George is partly spastic. This type of distortion is easily recognizable, and may explain why many paraplegics are not given job interviews:

Grossly distorted writing may have a simple explanation, and this should always be borne in mind. Before attempting to analyze such a sample, try to determine the circumstances under which it was written. The following examples appear alarming until we read the explanations about them.

Rough notes written under pressure of time, and with reluctance or boredom:

Letter written on a train:

several new order

Address written with a borrowed, scratchy pen on an old scrap of paper, resting on a pillar box:

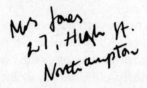

Mrs Jones
27, High St.
Northampton

Doctors' writing is mentioned several times in this book, and although there are doctors whose elegant, even handwriting survives the traumas of their profession, they are the exceptions. Such people are either naturally suited to working under tension, or are strongly gifted in other ways, tending possibly towards the visual arts. Most find their handwriting crumples under the unwelcome pressures of time and note-writing, and these characteristics are also typical of other over-worked professional people who, unlike most businessmen, do not generally thrive on pressure.

The following example demonstrates the conflict, rebellion, repression, impatience, exhaustion and self-denial so frequently found:

The regular use of antibiotic

1. Unfinished words show intelligence and impatience.
2. Right-pulled underloops show energy directed to the good of others.
3. Uneven upper loops prove constant disillusionment.
4. Irregular uprights reflect a conflict of loyalties between family and patient or client.
5. Variations in *t*-strokes show waxing and waning in drive and organizing ability, often due to tiredness.
These are a mild, or peripheral group of the symptoms of writer's

cramp, which, after fifty years of experimental research is now called writer's disturbance. Once all possible physical causes have been eliminated, this condition is thought to be symptomatic of a rebellion against the writing process, this often being linked to the writer's main occupation. It takes the form either of a persistent tremor in the script, ineffectual stabbing movements with the pen, or total paralysis of the hand *for writing purposes only*. Electric shocks successfully produce writing through fear, but it is hardly surprising that the victims of this condition retain no impulse to write, and this extinction of a conditioned reflex actually solves nothing. No graphologist can analyze what has not been written, but his view must surely be that this most extreme extension of distortion requires a total rest from writing and very probably a total change of occupation. Subsequently, all attempts at writing should be spontaneous. (This, after all, is the treatment for impotence.)

Grossly distorted writing is immediately disturbing to the reader, but the sometimes unique distortion of a single letter is a swift clue to character, and often a means of indentification.

The positioning and formation of (A)'s *s* is the most unusual feature of his writing.

(B)'s right-turned lower stroke is explained in the alphabetical lists, and shows energy used for others.

As (B)'s altruistic lower stroke shows, distortions can have a pleasant significance. Employers who have studied graphology soon learn to recognize those which, for their particular area of work, are most desirable in applicants' writing.

7. Changes

Changes in the writing show development and growth, or shrinking and disintegration. For initial investigation into changes within writing it is best to consider one's own, using a recent sample and one from several years ago.

Are there major or minor changes, or none at all? Your character has changed accordingly. If you find that your writing has changed within the past month or week then the answer is the same. If you find, however, that your writing changes within the scope of one piece of work, or within one letter to another person, then you will need to read the section on Conflict. Such changes are very sudden.

It is normal for confidence, drive, energy and health to fluctuate quite strongly, and the following variations may be noted within weeks or days.

Drooping *t*-strokes show tiredness or lack of drive:

settled

Downward-sloping lines of writing mean the same:

settled for you

Unfinished endings are a sign of impatience, haste or pressure of work:

necessary amount

(necessary amount)

The first of these *s*'s shows strength and independence, the second yielding and a desire to please:

S *ʂ*

They may alternate in the writing (see page 41).

Variation in size is chiefly proof of an adaptable nature, though one isolated small or large word suggests emotional involvement:

Jane is at Oxford now

Long term changes are of interest, but often merely confirm self-knowledge. Writing which has become unlinked, or less linked, shows a slackening of self-centred drive unless the linked script was enforced in earlier days (see page 21). It also shows a greater awareness of the pace and pattern of the writer's environment:

was eventually was eventually

Writing which has become more strongly linked shows an intensification of self-awareness and inner drive:

yesterday yesterday

A formerly upright hand which now slopes forward indicates a reaching-out towards others, and a greater need of them:

pastry is cooked pastry is cooked

A formerly upright hand which has now pulled backwards shows injury to the emotions. The new back-slope proves that a satisfactory modus vivendi has now been found, even though it is based on distrust of others:

looking forward looking forward

Writing which slopes in more than one direction shows present hurt. Lightened pressure indicates declining strength:

help to give help to give

Intensified pressure shows a greater capacity for tackling life:

promise that promise that

Writing which generally flows more evenly than before means that some of the problems of earlier years have been ironed out:

the whole thing the whole thing

Recently evolved jerkiness marks the onset of difficulties:

wait until you   to wait until you

These general changes, all of which relate to earlier chapters, are of immense importance in marriage guidance work. Such changes, after several years of marriage, are a barometer of its progress; the placing side by side of consecutive samples of writing will indicate what has happened.

Changes in the formation of certain letters can be interpreted through the alphabetical lists. Those which fluctuate constantly have already been indicated, but there are others which, whilst being by no means signs of maturity in the sense of increased wisdom, do tend to develop in the middle years, sometimes sooner:

The secretive *e*. This letter begins to close and becomes eyeless when its writer is living with a secret.

e

The lower loop may lose its self-gratifying leftward swing:

g

It may become short and hard, showing a repressed physical nature:

g

It may show anger or frustration:

It may indicate that the writer has channelled his energy into helping others:

It may indicate that the writer has channelled his energy into helping others:

The personal *I*, being very significant in expressing the self, may occasionally alter during the course of years. Here is a confident, self-accepting formation:

It may develop a self-protective curve quite early in life, or a dependence on parents:

A fear of becoming engulfed and unnoticed will produce bars above and below the *I* as a form of definition and self-projection:

Other forms of the personal *I* are discussed on pages 87-89. If there is a sudden change in its formation this may be a cause for anxiety, since a dramatic reassessment of the self after adolescence is unusual. Psychotherapy may produce changes within weeks, however, and such changes will normally be desirable. It is the sudden change which coincides with strange behaviour that is worrying. See the sections on Conflict, Diagnosis of Illness, and Criminal Detection.

If you are contemplating analyzing the handwriting of a teenager, please remember that sudden changes are all part of the programme of puberty. See the section on Understanding Teenagers at the beginning of Chapter V. I have covered some of the more common changes here, but it should be possible for you to analyze any alteration in your writing by using the alphabetical lists. Here is an example:

Expanded letter   becomes contracted.

Changes in the size of your writing will be connected with your pen, your eyesight, and what was acceptable on the page or in the days of your first sample compared with what is acceptable today. Other changes are far more significant, and only in exceptional cases will size indicate a dramatic change in character.

In the following section we discuss conflict. It has been placed last in the survey of First Impressions because understanding conflict in handwriting requires an acquaintance with the basics of graphology. It will be best to read it straight through and to return to it later than to try to apply it immediately in analysis.

8. Conflict

Most handwriting shows some degree of conflict within its creator's character: the indications are found in the stopping, gushing or opposing directions of the flow. Totally integrated or balanced writing springs only from a brain where there are no opposing impulses, but the strong conditioning forces of hereditary traits, parental ideals or discipline, and the accepted ways of our peers make this situation a rarity. Most of us have to compromise daily between what we have to (or feel we have to) do, and what we want to do.

Nevertheless, we should probably resent being described as in a state of conflict. For the purposes of this section we must differentiate between destructive conflict, which prevents the personality from fulfilling its potential, and the minor conflict which makes for an interesting and diversified character without causing self-injury. Minor conflict is shown in several ways, and one of these is a regular variation in the forming of certain letters. We have already discussed the lower case *s*.

When both types are regularly included the character has bursts of independence interspersed with yielding:

S ð

A wandering *i* dot shows a character torn between attending to minute details or facts, and taking a blatantly curious interest in the doings of other people:

.

i L

Very often one lower loop has a tendency to turn in a different direction from the others. Here there is conflict between giving and taking. See each lower case letter in the alphabetical lists, and the section on The Lower Case.

turning away

from you

Closed *a*'s and *o*'s sometimes keep company with very open ones. Here is someone who gossips freely about others while keeping his own affairs well concealed:

stay over

These are a few of the more common letter variations. The meanings of others may be found in the alphabetical lists, and it must be realized that they are both features of the personality.

Minor conflict is also shown in letter endings:

five ounces of
rice . Boil in
plenty of water
for fifteen mins.

This combination means one of two things, and other factors in the writing will decide which; either this is a stubborn person who at times becomes so absorbed in his occupation that he forgets to be defensive, or he is a mild person who occasionally digs in his heels. Check the pressure, *t*-strokes and *s*'s.

Come home

Hard, abrupt word endings indicate a character who must always have the last word. Other features may show him to be generous and easy-going.

Other signs of minor conflict are frequently found. Unnecessary loops in *d*'s and *t*'s appear from time to time in many people's writing, showing self-pity. These loops are small quantities of escaping emotion which plead, 'Please appreciate me', and are often found in the writing of self-disciplined, socially conscious people:

and have much

kind invitation

the dentist

Irregular use of the cautionary stroke shows a person who can be very rash when he is not using his normal checking tactics. He does not always stop to consider his next action, and there may be sharp contrasts in his behaviour:

you might like

A division between major and minor conflict may be made by the fact that whereas major conflict disrupts the entire flow of the writing, minor conflict is indicated by regular alternatives in stroke or letter formations. Such alternate formations show problems or divergent attitudes which the writer has learned to live with. He has converted and blended his conflicting impulses until they have come to form part of the pattern of his life. They do not disturb the coherence of the writing, nor the eye of the reader, because they do not greatly disturb their creator.

Major conflict or disruption of the personality is shown by a massive disturbance in the flow of the writing. We are not talking now of small disturbances which the writer has incorporated into the flow of his writing, but those which either halt the flow of the writing or make the component parts clash and collide:

(thing is making me want to go)

Such writing is immediately disturbing.

Repression, frustration and fear are strongly developed in conflict-ridden writing, and will be manifest in the part of the letter which relates to that part of the personality most affected:

away days   *very good*   *going away*

Lack of   Physical frustration   Physical repression
physical drive

Thick, hard, angular strokes, often intercrossing, indicate a character at war with itself. Do not confuse them with consistently heavy pressure:

giving   *giving*

Heavy pressure   Angry or interrupted flow

Conflicting strokes will appear abrupt or sawn off. There will not be a smooth and natural flow to the writing.

Vertical strokes which veer in different directions were discussed in the section on Slope. Such uneven uprights indicate emotional disturbance, and an ambivalent attitude to other people often connected with extreme emotional vulnerability:

perpendicular style

It would be helpful to turn back now and find both this and physical repression evident in the first sample of writing containing gross conflict.

Such writing will demonstrate uneven flow in its alternate bursts of expanded or contracted middle case writing. Sometimes the letters have a broad, loosely controlled flow, whilst at others they are tight and angular:

taken a long time

Often there will be signs of encroachment, followed by self-correction:

very many thanks

Where there is positive enjoyment of encroachment the character is unbalanced or dis-integrated. See The Balance of the Personality.

very many thanks

Conflict in graphological terms means double impulse. Sometimes this is found in alternate light and hard pressure, which within one writing sample, as opposed to within the writing of different weeks or months, can indicate quite serious disturbance in the brain:

the only one

Before making any such analysis please re-read the section on Pressure and discover the situation in which the letter was written. As in distorted writing, there may be a simple explanation for a disturbed writing pattern, but just occasionally its presence will confirm a worry already present; professional help should then be sought at once. (No professional adviser will take offence at a query, though he may if told an opinion.)

   Conflict in the writing of people aged between twelve and twenty or so is discussed in Understanding Teenagers. At no time is conflict so painful or so easy to relieve as during adolescence. When an older person has difficulty in choosing between several writing styles it is usually because he is aware of two or more irreconcilable persona in his character. People tell me emphatically that they have two separate writing styles: sometimes they do, but more often only one aspect, such as slope, is actually different:

The Statute   The statute

When the two samples differ in many ways the writer is happy to tell me about his two 'selves'. This often amounts to no more than the wearing of two different hats, and Mrs Clark is a good example of the syndrome. She is an infants' teacher and needs a simple and legible form of writing for use in school; at other times she allows her natural brain flow to dominate:

making our beds   making our beds

There is frequently a sensible explanation for the use of two styles, and even when there is not the writer can usually put a label to each one, and give a happy description of that 'self'.

It is only when a writer either shows anxiety about his two handwriting styles, or is unwilling to let me see them, that I suspect severe conflict. Once conflict has been acknowledged, aired and analyzed it is possible for it to be alleviated, but the character who denies the existence of inner conflict cannot be helped, may hurt himself or others, and sadly will move from the scope of this chapter to the area of disturbance covered by Diagnosis of Illness.

Gross conflict is shown by complete upheaval in the writing, which will vary in size, slope, letter formation, line slope and positioning on the page. Its component parts may clash as previously described. The writer will be under severe mental pressure, but no personality disorder is indicated unless other factors, discussed in Diagnosis of Illness, are present.

the only one I have ever wanted is no use in the

The forms of conflict shown in the sample above and discussed fully in this section are all capable of amateur understanding and help. Once a neurotic problem has been admitted to, the writer is usually capable of tackling it, and the section which starts Chapter V, Self-help — Reversing the Flow, may help. Psychotherapy has been described as the slow acceptance of unpalatable home truths, and to a limited extent graphology can speed up the process.

One area of conflict which can at once be isolated from the scope of mental disturbance is emotional distress. It is shown when the writing contains *no other signs of major conflict but unparallel uprights*:

perpendicular style

Emotional conflict affects only emotional relationships, and the brain is not disordered unless there are other signs present. It cannot be dangerous to others, but if severe depression or lack of self-respect is indicated, it may be dangerous to the individual himself. More often emotional conflict *by itself* can be alleviated by gentle discussion with family or friends.

On this premise it is acceptable for a learner graphologist to claim to recognize emotional disturbance, but not to make pronouncements on any other form of mental disturbance. At this point it would be interesting to re-examine (B)'s handwriting on page 9.

9. Left-Handedness

For several years I conducted independent research into left-handedness, pouncing on friends who write thus and subjecting them to every kind of experiment. I used my understanding of their characters as I had experienced it in their behaviour, and compared it with the traits expressed in their writing, and was eventually forced to the conclusion that left-handedness had no bearing on graphology: such writers are subject to the same rules of flow as those who use their right hand.

Among the questions I asked was this: would they prefer to write from right to left across the page? The answer was no, although it was pointed out that this would avoid the dragging of the wrist through newly applied wet ink. In no respect could I find conflict between the brain flow of a left-handed writer and the accepted writing patterns of a right-handed majority. Without exception, resentment was confined to memories of those who had tried to make them write with their non-preferred hand. All remembered unhappy incidents in early childhood when their tendency to become left-handers had been noticed and discouraged, and only one had managed to make the change.

Some graphologists impute a significance to left-handedness itself. I find that I cannot. But I retain an open mind, and should welcome positive information from those readers who are best placed to give it; the left-handed.

II
Letter Formations

1. Using the Alphabetical Lists

We now come to the analysis of individual letters. As we have already found, few facets of handwriting can be interpreted in isolation, and before imputing any of the brief character studies which accompany each letter, please make sure there are four or five examples of that formation in the writing.

Quite often more than one form of a certain letter is found, the *s* and *g* being common examples of this:

S ♪ ዋ *g*

Read all the relevant interpretations, remembering that one person is capable of taking more than one attitude.

In the formation of individual letters the emphasis on each particular stroke is as important as the shape of the letter as a whole. If the letter formation you are seeking is apparently absent, you will need to return to Emphasis (see below) since you will now have to analyze the component parts, and discover the significance of each separate stroke. This, indeed, is the way the alphabetical lists were compiled, and you will not be able to claim to be a graphologist until you have a thorough understanding of that process.

2. Emphasis

When the explanation for a letter formation cannot be found in the alphabetical lists, the following principles of emphasis must be applied. Letters with upper or lower strokes or loops receive special attention in Chapter III, The Balance of the Personality.

To investigate emphasis we must follow the letter formation along its natural course, from left to right. Does it begin firmly, like this book print, or does it have a preliminary or cautionary stroke?

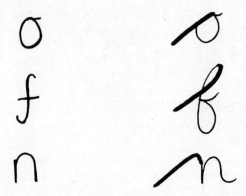

Such strokes are not always joining strokes, nor are they decorations or embellishments unless quite separately formed (see page 32). When they appear at the beginning of a word or on a free-standing letter they indicate a dragging of the pen whilst the brain hesitates before committing itself to paper. If the letter you seek resembles the one shown in the alphabetical lists in all other respects but the cautionary stroke, or the lack of it, then you may accept the explanation given, adding or subtracting the factor of caution. The longer the preliminary stroke the greater is the deliberation whilst writing. Such writers also tend to make their initial indecision obvious in their actions.

People who have no cautionary strokes in their writing are not necessarily rash. They tend to think out a plan of action privately before embarking on a project, which makes them appear more decisive. Rashness is shown when the pen joins all the letters in one word without lifting, and may follow an initial cautionary stroke. (An executive who writes thus is less open to reason than his counterpart who has no cautionary strokes but leaves small gaps between the letters.)

The first downstroke of the letter relates to purposefulness and domination. It will be seen that the cautionary stroke can have a modifying effect on this, especially when it is in itself a broad, heavy movement.

In other cases, however, the cautionary stroke is merely a long, lingering run up before bowling, with the emphasis of the letter falling on the first downstroke.

Try to determine where the main emphasis of the letter lies. It may be a heavier, longer or straighter stroke than the others. If it involves an upper or lower case formation refer to pages 139-141.

If there is a second downstroke to the letter and it bears a heavier emphasis than the first this points to a degree of neurosis or fear:

If you are analyzing an upper or lower case stroke see page 141.

Emphasis on the upstrokes is a sign of a tendency towards imaginative thinking, and is also found in conjunction with other signs of idealism (see page 144). Overemphasis on the cautionary stroke has a similar meaning, since it is also an upstroke:

Upper loops are treated separately on page 143, but the emphasis is still normally downwards:

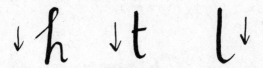

Strong emphasis on the final stroke of the letter, especially at the end of a word, indicates stubbornness, usually caused by fear:

Where the stroke is incomplete or shorter, over-confidence or impatience is shown:

This can be interpreted as fast-thinking speedwriting in an otherwise intelligent hand. Words begin clearly enough but tail away into nothing, and each unfinished word says, 'I've already made my point and you should have grasped it by now. I'm going on to the next point.' This is a common facet of doctors' handwriting; making notes is often an irritation and not what they feel they are there for. See also signatures which drift away into nothing (page 175).

   Strokes which connect words were dealt with in the section on Flow.

   Light writing will often show apparently equal emphasis. It will appear thus in the handwriting of some musicians and artists, the former in small floating letters resembling musical notes, and the latter in well-formed painted letters as shown on page 52. The emphasis may not be obvious, but it is there. See page 19 for other signs of a musical nature.

The slow, laborious writing of the very unintelligent person may certainly contain equal emphasis. This is due to lack of impulsion from the brain: the act of writing is an effort and the script does not flow:

Watch for broken letter strokes. Except in floating *t*-bars (page 118-119) or in capital letters these can be signs of illness, especially heart trouble. Make sure you can recognize them; they have breaks in them where the pen has left the paper at an unnatural point (see page 219).

h   c   p   t

They are not the same as unfinished letters:

a   o   b

or painted letters:

paint

Unfinished letters show an over-relaxed, uncaring attitude. Painted letters are often beautiful and a sign of visual ability; the section on Flow should have implanted an awareness of this. Letters which appear unique are occasionally found. They owe their appearance to under- or overemphasis, and can seem at first as unrecognizable as Chinese or Russian letters:

s   e   y   M

Try to determine the emphases before reading the explanations which follow.

The writer of *s* cannot achieve the individuality or independence he desires, nor will he yield to others; he is thus left with no alternative but to dig in his heels and avoid confrontations altogether. Such a characteristic shows the reverse of fulfilment.

The writer of *e* is in a hurry to move on to the next idea. He is probably intelligent but impatient.

The writer of *y* has much to contribute to the good of others, but he does it at the expense of his own personality balance. This formation relates to underloops (see page 151).

The writer of *M* has never found life easy. His own impulses are generally overriden by a strong sense of duty, and he does not understand why other people do not behave in the same way. He often feels neglected and depressed, but nevertheless is probably a person to contend with, as the attempt at a stubborn ending shows.

The current interest in electro-encephalographic patterns corresponds with the notion that there is an ideal, that is, a calm and fulfilled, rhythm of emphasis in any individual's writing. This pattern, together with the flow, will be disrupted by conflict or malfunction. It is the graphologist's task to find the sites and possible causes of disruption.

3. Capital Letters

Our early schooldays imprint a sense of occasion and importance into the writing of any capital letter. We defer to the word which begins with a capital either because it is a proper noun or because it begins a new thought.

Some people do not choose to defer, and if unenlarged letters such as follow are caused deliberately rather than in error, then we are dealing with a rebel:

(See pages 99 and 231.)

Other writers expand the importance of the capital, making it far larger than necessary. This may apply to a few formations only, or it may only happen in certain writing situations: it shows a desire for pattern and order in life. It may also show respect for and acceptance of authority, especially in writing where the terminal *s* is a yielding one (see page 115), and where there are signs of self-control (loopless upper and lower strokes). In other writing exaggerated capitals may indicate that the authority most respected is the writer's own, but this is rare. Initials in signatures are discussed from page 169; over-tall capitals on page 99.

Immense personal and emotional involvement influences the

formation of the capital '*I*' and '*M*'. It is quite possible that other capitals such as personal initials are significant in the writer's life, and here the emphasis will be distorted or over-loaded. Emotional significance may also account for enlarged capitals, or for abrupt final downstrokes indicating defensiveness or fear.

Investigation of many handwriting samples shows that there is a pattern of joined or unjoined capitals. For instance, the *T* may always stand alone whilst the *S* is always joined to the next letter. This pattern only has meaning if the direction of the joining stroke is considered, unless an emotional link with the letter itself has caused an abrupt withdrawal.

Central join:

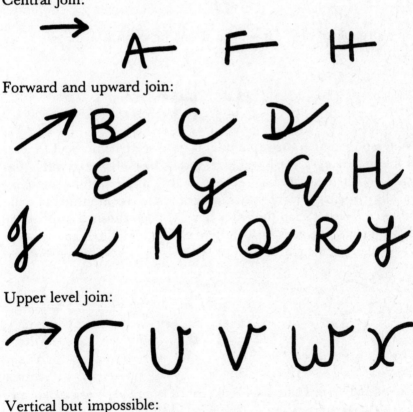

Forward and upward join:

Upper level join:

Vertical but impossible:

Leftward — impossible:

← O P D B

The formation of a capital letter may be altered to accommodate a joining stroke of a certain angle. This forward and upward stroke is a time-saving device for the impatient, onward-driving extrovert. He will incorporate many such strokes in his writing:

The organizer of ideas will join on the central level wherever possible:

A H

When one joining direction only is used see Diagnosis of Illness. Joining strokes on the lower level should be interpreted with great care. When the letter has been carefully completed first, a joining stroke from left to right shows integration and contentment on the physical level. When the letter has not been finished impatience is indicated. See page 181, if there is an attempt to create a lower case where none exists.

Completed, joined letter.   Unfinished letter.   False lower case.

Consider the emphasis of a capital letter which stands totally alone:

Psychic

The *P* is calmly and slowly written, and is followed by a pause as the writer plans the spelling of a difficult word.

Emotional involvement, probably in the whole word. Note the hiccup as the pen leaps upward, indicating fear, anxiety, anger or excitement.

The embellishment of capital letters is almost always caused by vanity or self-projection, but remember to distinguish between decorations, which are extra, additional or grossly extended strokes, and distortions, which are malformed strokes within the main body of the letter.

Decorated capital letter.   Distorted capital letter.

If the letter you are examining is part of a signature, see pages 175-185 before making a judgement, and study illegible signatures, cyphers, decorations, and marks of self-defence. Whenever a capital letter shows a strange or divergent pattern within the writing, ask whether it has a particular significance in the writer's life.

4. Alphabetical Lists

a

A careful formation with or without the cautionary stroke. It shows manual dexterity and discretion.

This is the 'open mouth' which is sometimes indiscreet or careless, but open and honest. See the section on Conflict for combined use of this and the character below.

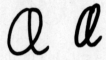

This formation is the reverse of that above, for here strong feelings are kept in check. The narrower the formation, the more likely the writer is to have secrets of his own, which, since he is naturally demonstrative, is a strain. (See page 155.)

Here is secrecy verging on deception.

Soft, short endings indicate impatience. Hard short or long endings show stubbornness, the former dismissive, the latter persistent.

This is a decorated formation, done for artistic effect. See page 183 if it occurs in a signature. Its backward facing stance shows a preoccupation with past events or values.

There is distortion in this upward-pulled formation. Check to see if there is a general overhead pull in the writing (see page 154). If not, this must count as a lazy or unfinished letter.

This letter has been made square as part of a pattern. The effort in every letter shows a character more dependent on his home environment than on other people.

A

There are few variants from the classic print-type *A*, but this is the most common, showing organizing ability on the logical/practical level.

This is the *A* taught as a correct capital formation in schools from time to time. It enables a continuous linking of all the letters in the word. Those who learned this at school and still use the same formation are likely to conform in most respects to the ways in which they were brought up.

Here is an attempt at producing a vertical letter. Such a writer is independent in nature but is also concerned about being seen to be so. The initial stroke is a post to hold the A upright.

Round topped A's are often a feature of generally rounded or arched writing, indicating protectiveness, caring, and a tendency to treat any situation with a strong personal bias.

Strokes which return to touch other parts of the letter show a compulsion to double-check facts and figures. When the backward-joined t-stroke is also present this indicates a slightly obsessional aspect to the personality.

b

A classically formed b, whether joined in front and behind or not, shows a character who takes the time and trouble to do things properly.

This is a painted *b*, produced by someone with creative, visual or artistic talent.

Additional loops are always escaping emotion, but less so in a hand where they are not present in the *d* or *t*. Very tall loops indicate religious, philosophical or idealistic interests. (See page 144.)

This writer is being driven onwards by his own brain impulsion. It is an unfinished letter caused by impatience, but the writer is probably intelligent.

This inverted formation is traditionally associated with dyslexia, and when word-inversion is also present, this is probably the reason for its appearance. It may, however, indicate a psychological condition. (See page 197).

This shows a conforming nature, or great respect for one's parents, since it is basically a schoolroom formation.

b b

Upper strokes which are either abruptly curtailed or are short and weak are discussed on pages 142-144.

B

B

B is a time-consuming letter to write, and those who form it perfectly are those who like to do all things correctly. It also shows manual dexterity.

B

Joining on the lower level indicates a practical and pragmatic nature.

B

This is a painted letter, usually indicating a visually gifted person, but when it is found in a sample of generally heavy or strongly linked writing it shows unwillingness to complete the letter. It is then a sign of laziness.

There is complex motivation in this letter form. The writer is cautious, painstaking to the point of obsession, yet with a strong practical drive. There may well be other signs of conflict or self-dissatisfaction in the writing, such as a tendency to go back and correct badly formed letters.

c

A long cautionary stroke as always indicates thought before action, but this is part of an upward curve which is often repeated in waves throughout the writing. It shows an upward pull, into thoughtfulness.

This *c* is the reverse in emphasis, drawing away from the higher part of the brain into the lower. (See page 24.)

Here the base of the letter lingers on the lower level, finalizing practical details and not rising until absolutely necessary.

This highly controlled formation shows manual dexterity.

C

The upper wave is an extension of the upward curve. If it rises above most of the other middle case letters see page 50, but if it merely lowers the letter form it should be regarded as a loop. (See below.)

Loops which intrude where they should not show exposed emotion and lack of control, but in fast flowing even writing with no upper loops this is probably the sole outlet of a highly self-disciplined nature.

This slow formation is seldom seen now, but embodies discretion and a sense of propriety. (See Victorian writing on page 136.)

d

A carefully formed letter showing self-control or manual dexterity.

Loops in *d* uprights are exposed emotion, showing a need for affection and understanding. Such self-pity may be transitory. (See page 145.)

In the middle of a word greater dexterity is needed to make this movement neatly. It requires a calm, orderly mind or great manual skill.

A strong attempt is being made here to refine and uplift the mind, but loneliness is still evident, probably only in the *d* and *t* uprights. (See page 144.)

This writer does not permit his upright stroke to extend to its correct height, showing an earthy outlook on life. (See Emphasis and page 142.)

This Greek *d* is often found in the writing of artists and those with an unmaterialistic vision. Above all, it is backward leaning, showing a preoccupation with past events and values. (See page 145.)

This inverted formation is traditionally associated with dyslexia, and when word-inversion is also present, this is probably the reason for its appearance. It may, however, indicate a psychological condition. (See page 197.)

This is a high-joined formation, showing fast, imaginative thinking at some cost to idealism (see page 145) and discretion, (open top as in the open *a*).

This is an unfinished letter, and as above, is caused by impatience. However, it may combine with other traits in the writing to suggest fatigue and conflict, for there is control in the *d*-upright and none in the open top. (See above.)

This is not an unfinished letter, but a painted one, showing a visual conception of life.

For a rightward bent upper stroke (see page 146).

This downward plunging upright may indicate one of several things. If all the word endings are long and hard, stubbornness and persistence are shown, but it is more likely to be a compensatory lower case stroke. (See page 182.)

D

This *D* starts with a cautionary stroke but is left unfinished in its strong rightward turn. It has been formed more as a decoration than as a fast-flowing letter.

Painstaking application and a desire to please are shown here.

Here is a strong pull towards the lower case. (See page 182, especially if this is part of a signature.) The preliminary stroke shows caution.

This subtle formation shows a powerful mind and strong drive. Its initial painted stroke shows a sure, visual concept, and its height, ideas at work.

Here is a similar powerful mind actioned by slower, pragmatic thinking. (See Victorian writing on page 136.)

This distorted but undecorated D also shows several functions of the brain working together. There is some conflict in the upper left then rightward turn. (See page 100.)

This is a painted letter, showing a visual or perceptionist view of life. (Refer to page 20.)

This decorated letter indicates a deliberate showman's attitude, especially if used in a signature. It is also visually gifted, as above.

e

e e

A well-balanced *e* has a closed hole in the upper half, and shows tolerance, honesty and discretion.

ε ∈

The Greek *e* is a rare alternative found in the writing of those who consciously seek a cultivated or artistic way of life. There can be undertones of contempt for accepted standards, but for this to be true there must also be unenlarged capitals and dwindling word endings.

This formation is over-closed and eye-shaped, indicating more discretion than honesty.

This is an extension of the above *e*, and here there is a secret. The writer is concealing an important fact in his life, and there will frequently be other signs of strain in the writing.

This trailing *e* shows a reluctance to move on, or an uncertainty that all is well behind him. When linked with closed *s*'s and expansive writing (page 154) it indicates a yielding character, but with hard pressure and open *s*'s, tenacity.

Here no attempt has been made to form the letter. The writer is driven forward on the upper thinking level, and is probably very intelligent, but if consistent this is still a sign of secrecy.

Closed formation. See the closed *c* on page 63. Some manual dexterity is shown.

Here the emphasis is in the understroke rather than the downstroke and shows an uncompromising nature. If the words end consistently with this stroke, the writer has a stubborn nature.

E

The loops in the top and in the centre of this capital show escaping emotion. Although it is a yielding formation it is self-centred (see page 136 and page 155).

This distorted formation may be reflected throughout the writing, and if so it suggests an unusual balance between logic and instinct. If in the *E* alone, especially in the signature, it is a decoration.

€

See lower case *e* on page 69.

f

f

This is a painted letter, formed by two strokes with a sudden deft movement of the hand. Only when the central bar joins on to the next letter is it a connected, organizer's formation. (See page 119.)

f

This is also a painted letter, but it stands on the line and has no lower case. In light writing it suggests musical or artistic ability i.e., sensitivity in the central part of the brain pattern.

The schoolroom *f* of years ago shows a conforming nature, and a sense of duty. (See Victorian writing on page 136.)

f

This formation is similar to that above, but with self-pity built into it. (See page 155.)

This backward facing *f* is related to the similar capital on page 74, but in moving on to join the next letter forms a tightly controlled lower loop. This shows physical yielding and acceptance.

There is anger and frustration here. Physical activities do not give satisfaction: a resistance against real or imagined bullying is indicated, and much strength is being repressed.

This is an accentuation of the above *f*, with repressed strength bursting into self-pity. There may be restrained violence in this hand, especially when the uprights are uneven and the whole middle case criss-crosses. (See page 224.)

F

All capital letters which are plain and undecorated show that the writer prefers life to be simple and honest, even if his own nature prevents it from being so.

This is a painted formation. (See page 20.) It shows an imaginatively visual concept, but if the *t*-bars also fly ahead of the upright, the writer is allowing his ideas to run away with him.

A backward-turned *F* looks to the past for inspiration and confirmation. This is especially true when used in the word *From*, when used consistently in this and other letters, and where there is no joining stroke.

If the stroke which connects the base with the central stroke is light, this is a similar *F* to the backward facing one on page 73 but includes anger over real or supposed oppression.

This is the organizer's centrally joining stroke.

g

The classic lower case *g* is surprisingly rarely found. This letter requires at least four turns of the wrist to complete it, and it is important that it should end softly, showing physical fulfilment. (See page 147.)

Here physical self-indulgence is over-extended, cutting through the middle case. (See page 150.)

Here is great physical capacity and strength, controlled and co-ordinated into a typical 'sportsman's' elongated underloop.

This is another frustrated curve, or jarred understroke. The writer is not finding physical satisfaction, although he has a strong capacity for enjoyment.

This understroke shows intense physical repression. It has been abruptly curtailed, but the dotted lines show the strength and possible fulfilment of this writer's physical potential. (See page 141.)

This understroke is both frustrated and angry. See the similar understrokes on the letter *f*.

Here is a physical strength which has been put to no purpose. It may be in a state of flux, about to turn in a new direction at its base, showing a different channelling of energy.

q

This understroke is beginning to turn right, showing energy directed to the good of others. The *g* is often the only letter in the writing to have such an understroke, showing one facet of a physically subtle nature.

q

Here is the committed, and happy, altruistic rightward turn. Note the soft, fulfilled ending.

q

Unless all the letters appear to be decorated this jarred understroke shows an unnatural social conscience, possibly formed by school or parents. The writer should review the expenditure of his energy.

This writer is able to give both to himself and to others physically. The lower loop should be neither pulled tight (excessive control), nor allowed to spread into the central case as on page 150.

Here altruism and good deeds have taken over the personality and stunted its capability for physical enjoyment. See page 147 for interpretations of short, weak or soft endings.

G

The formation of this *G* requires slow care, and its writers are those who like to see a good practical job well done.

This writer has created an understroke, and thereby added a physical dimension. The direction and strength of the capital *G* understroke is of great interest, since it shows a voluntary physical bias. (See pages 147-8.)

This is a backward-looking, emotionally charged letter. It shows a reasoning personality who has known happier times.

Here is deliberately projected frustration; almost a cry for help. Remember that the *G* does not need an understroke, so this is a gratuitous physical expression.

Although all capital *G* understrokes are in a sense decorations, this is almost a drawing of physical conflict and tension. The writer has a problem and we must turn to pages 147-8 to assess it.

Here is deliberate balancing. This is an unashamedly emotional, physically happy person who is prepared to accept the consequences of his nature.

This is another emotional pendulum swing. Read all the *G* interpretations to see its significance.

The capital *G*, when found in spontaneous script and not written
for the graphologist, is an excellent test of true physical bias. (See
pages 147-8.)

h

All uprights which exclude loops show controlled feelings. When
the upright is of reasonable height and the hump more or less round,
a balanced character is indicated.

Here there is an upper loop which does not extend very high,
showing emotional demonstrativeness.

The loop has the above significance. A flattened *h* hump is traditionally associated with an immature attitude towards spending money. The writer does not bring his brain into play and may be a miser or a spendthrift — or both.

This writer applies principles to all his actions and emotions. We know this from the upward pull, and the slim loop. (See page 144.)

Here is repression in the upper case. Where the upright stops abruptly there is lack of fulfilment, where softly, lack of interest in idealism. (See page 141.)

This *h* is by nature shorthand or speedwriting. By omitting the hump the writer is hastening an idea through without thinking round it. (See page 53.)

This could be interpreted as financial neurosis, for it shows emotional anxiety in the logical thinking area, without higher influence.

Here is emotional idealism, linked with socially defensive thinking. Much attention must be paid to the rest of the writing before judging, since in itself this is clearly out of balance.

This is the writing of someone under mental pressure. Generosity of a practical kind is seen in the high, widening hump. (See page 146.)

H

Calm and self-control is indicated by a perfectly formed *H*. Slight deviations in the length of strokes are due only to manual ineptitude, but differing angles in the uprights are significant. (See page 15.)

This stroke shows obsessional double checking. The writer has a compulsion to return to ground already covered, and this stroke will probably occur frequently in the writing.

Here is a retrospective loop of emotion in the middle case. If the centre stroke of the letter joins on to the next, the formation is obsessional as above; if not, it shows a tendency to dwell on practical problems.

This formation appears to be decorated, but in reality shows an unusual vision linking all parts of the brain. Although there is neurosis, it is put to creative use.

This is the organizer's centrally based joining stroke.

This is a decorated letter. Double strokes like this often spring from a musician's brain, but are nevertheless created initially for effect. (See page 69.)

Here the very low-based joining stroke is attempting to reach into the lower, physical, case. If this movement is consistent throughout the writing, see page 182.

The gap in this *H* shows a mal- or non-function of the logical part of the brain: such formations may be found in the writing of elderly or absent-minded people. The small loops show emotion and anxiety concerning both the past and the future, and the hooked base indicates physical difficulties.

Emphasis on the second half of the letter shows lack of self-trust. (See the similar *M* on page 100.)

H may be a maleable and variable formation. If the one you seek is not here, re-read Emphasis.

i

This letter may be joined or not, so pay no attention to the foot of the upright. Dots consistently placed close to the downstroke show application to detail.

A dot consistently placed just ahead of the downstroke shows an active, thinking brain.

Dots high in the sky show an absorbed interest in the doings of other people. When they alternate with very accurate dotting they show a gregarious student. The reader will soon be able to make such assessments himself.

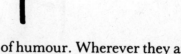

Flicked *i* dots show a sense of humour. Wherever they are placed, this is something to look for in applicants' writing when the job involves working with the general public.

Here the brain makes use of humour and links it to ideas/satire.

Dots which are placed consistently behind the downstroke show a slow, but thorough brain.

This is a deliberate attempt to be different. The writer does not mind being described as zany or eccentric, and refuses to allow his life to become boring. (See the signature on page 183.)

This *i* signifies what it suggests; a lack of attention to detail, or forgetfulness.

Random *i* dotting is uncommon among mature adults, whereas a pattern of two differing *i* dots is frequently found.

Dots which vary their position to this extent show a distracted mind.

I

The importance of the capital *I* in analysis will at once be appreciated. Because it refers to the self we hope to find it formed consistently throughout the writing, and of moderate size, neither disproportionately large nor shrivelled. This letter has special reference to all sections in Chapter V.

Whatever other signs of insecurity are found in the writing this person basically accepts his own nature, and expects other people to accept it, too. When its size, slope and pressure match the rest of the writing it points to a happy disposition.

This writer accepts himself, but anticipates criticism from others with these frame-like bars which say, 'You *will* take me as I am.' Bars well away from the upright add emphasis to this.

J

There is wariness here, and a measure of self-protection in the cautionary stroke. This writer will not always act spontaneously, and other letters as well as the signature may point to defensive tendencies.

g

Here is excessive discretion and unwillingness to expose the self. The final curl of the letter almost joins up with the first stroke. The loop in the upper or middle case indicates strong, concealed emotion.

7

This shows forethought, but also anger and frustration. The jarred protective strokes imply that however much care the writer puts into his actions, he is almost always denied fulfilment. Compare lower case strokes.

2

This formation is the slightly defended *I* of the previous page, with an added lower based rightward turn or joining stroke. If there is a downward pull this is an attempt to make a lower case addition to the letter. (See page 137.)

Here is defensive framing. This writer is basically happy with his nature, but like the earlier framer, he has come to expect others to question him. Unsympathetic schooling or home discipline will produce this formation.

The letter *I*, representing the self, will naturally be full of idiosyncrasies. Some formations will take the most experienced graphologist time to analyze, and the reader must expect to gain a thorough understanding of the three cases (Chapter III), as well as the section on Emphasis, before he can undertake them.

j

The small *j* does not necessarily require a dot, therefore the addition of one shows a painstaking attitude, or an admiration of things done correctly. (See page 147, The Lower Case.)

See above regarding dotting. The long slim 'sportsman's' underloop shows physical strength and co-ordination.

The frustration or anger felt by this writer may account for the lack of a dot, although (read above) one is not necessary. The loop above is contained emotion, showing physical problems approaching the mental area. (See page 152.)

Here is an unusual combination particularly if the *j*'s are always carefully dotted, and the underloops always as projected. I would expect either the attention to detail (precise dot), or the physical self-indulgence (large encroaching underloop) to dominate in any one writing sample.

This is not a lower case stroke, but a backward looking curl on the mental level. This writer remembers the past as holding his life's happiness. He would like to live for others but finds he cannot: it brings no fulfilment.

J

Here is an enthusiastic and (at least for the moment) altruistic *j*, with cautionary stroke but no dot. This is a good example of how easy analysis is when you know how to look at the letter formation.

This is a well-protected, physically expressed but controlled capital *J*. Many names begin with *J*, so look for this in signatures. (See page 136 on Victorian letter formations.)

Here is cheerful acceptance of frustration. The writer progresses as well as he can in physically trying circumstances.

k

This *k* (left) requires at least one lifting of the pen, and may be painted. Many variations of this and the following *k* will be found, the only difference between them being that the top is empty or joined in a loop. Visual writers, as above, are motivated by the shape and order of things, loop-makers by their feelings.

This high reaching *k* shows a tendency towards the higher planes of thinking. The loop shows that emotion sometimes accompanies these thoughts.

K

The capital *K* must be left open at the top or it becomes an *R*. It should thus be carefully formed with three separate strokes, but character will produce the following distortions.

This writer has reduced it to two strokes, and the ending may well join up with the next letter. This a part of fast script, and a bored or tired hand overlaps the downstroke at times besides, as it does here, missing it.

This is a fast-written *K* with a downward (physical) pull. Read the earlier *K* descriptions.

This writer, on the other hand, manages to create five separate strokes. But the letter is never properly formed: see the similar *H* on page 84.

Here is speedwriting of an intelligent kind. The writer will not allow his pen to leave the paper, and he has actually formed a loop. However, there must be many more looped letter formations in the writing before this is considered as such, since it is so obviously a time-saving device. (For backward loops see page 137.)

l

Loops in the small *l* show uncontrolled emotion, but the size of the loop modifies this. A very tall slim loop (left) shows emotion linked with a higher plane of thinking, see page 144. Low loops (centre and right), scarcely higher than the middle case, indicate emotion socially linked. The *l* is the natural place for loops; when they appear here, but not in the *d* or *t*, an affectionate nature is shown.

Small *l*'s without loops show a factual, thinking motivation, but they are only calm if they are all parallel. (See page 155.) Very high-reaching strokes show interest in idealism, philosophy or religion.

This *l* is linked and held on both sides to its accompanying letters. Its blunt top shows that it could be projected still further, but it is held back. The rest of the writing must be taken into consideration here. (See page 141.)

This formation has a weak upstroke and shows no interest in the higher planes of thinking. (See page 142.)

L

A capital *L* with straight strokes shows a realistic nature. However a truly straight base line is found only in the hands of those with an earthy, practical mind.

This swinging formation shows a character which acts on principle, is influenced by strong feelings and by the past, and which applies generous and practical attitudes simultaneously. All this will explain the old wives' tale about people with 'pound note' *L* formations! Such a character probably does enjoy handling and dispensing money. (See page 137.)

This is a similar formation with far more control. It is uninvolved emotionally (no loops) but operates on a thoughtful and responsible level. The hump in the baseline shows the leavening of principle in a practical matter.

Here the *L* climbs sharply away from the base, its brief, imaginative formation hastening on to the next thought.

There is always a link between the formation of the capital *L* and the small *h*. Both refer to the writer's attitude to money.

m

This evenly curved formation with its controlled lead-in and lack of loops shows an affectionate but emotionally aware personality.

Here is an even more efficient emotional watchdog, especially if this formation comes at the beginning of a word.

In this character emotion is allowed full play and demonstration. Though affection is given, response and interaction are always needed.

Here is a generous, artless giver of affection, though there is emotional independence and much common sense in this low-based, expansive handwriting.

If this plunging ending is a strong feature in the writing, then a slightly neurotic, stubborn persistence is in evidence. If it is found solely in the signature, refer to page 182.

Here is an angular formation, showing a tendency towards ideas and facts rather than people. (See page 155.)

There is an upper pull in this writing, showing the linking of ideas. It is basically contracted, emotionally undemonstrative writing, but the writer will take more interest in feelings than the previous character.

Here is a strong refusal to be involved emotionally, mainly through an awareness of personal vulnerability. Look carefully at the rest of the writing, especially the angle of the uprights.

This writer's character shows a mixture of common sense and logic. He is unlikely to be emotionally demonstrative, and may be lonely.

M

The capital *M* is uniquely revealing, and its inclusion is essential in any sample of handwriting for analysis. The formation of this letter appears to involve us emotionally to a considerable degree. During our earliest attempts at writing it was woven into 'Mummy', 'me' and 'my', and as we grew older it began to assume the shape of our own attitude towards ourselves and others. Many facets of our writing change from year to year, but surprisingly few *M*'s change or grow away from the early image of ourselves unless we have undergone radical psychotherapy.

We must examine this letter closely in order to assess our own handling of its writer, since it divulges personal attitudes which may never be openly displayed.

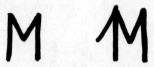

The cool, classic *M* (left). Unfettered by subjective prejudice, this writer accepts both people and facts on their obvious merits and does not endow them, or himself, with imagined characteristics. He is reasonable, and would make a good employer or employee, but look at his lower loops, *d*'s and *t*'s before marrying him. His clear-sighted vision could prove ruthlessly critical. A cautionary stroke will moderate this character (right).

This is what I call the 'mother hen'; well-balanced, affectionate and protective, with sufficient self-respect to stay calm, but no desire to dominate. Note that the first five of these capital *M*'s all carry equal emphasis on the two humps of the letter, indicating self-knowledge. Very round writing shows an affectionate nature.

An original, visual concept of life. Here, where the upper bar loses touch with its supports, we find someone who is idealistic to the point of losing touch with reality. This writer will fight for self-expression and have faith in his own artistic judgement, but will consider the attitudes of others. This is not a decorated letter in that there are no embellishments, but see The Upper Case on page 143.

Any letter which reaches to the sky shows an idealistic mental approach, but if the letter collides with the line above, or if the capital *M* stands above the level of its own line, as here, then the writer is given to flights of fancy. The cautionary stroke strengthens this character, and we must check with the other upper case letters and the *t*-strokes (see pages 117-20) to see if he is a fanatic.

A capital letter of lower case size is equally unrealistic and shows a desire to deny the commonly accepted influences of life such as parents, religion, status or authority. Taken in conjunction with linked *i* dots (page 86) it shows a satirical outlook, and with other features in the writing could have an artistic basis, but with slow, dragging writing of equal overall height it shows a stubborn, rootling mentality. (See page 23.)

Emphasis on the first half of the *M* shows pride and self-assurance, and is often found in the hand of those born into families of distinction. These people have an innate sense of their own importance and need to be handled firmly. Having asssessed other aspects of the writing such as the *s* and *d* we may assume them to be strongly self-confident, if not arrogant.

A cautionary lead-in (see page 49) only makes these people tougher, since they are unlikely to behave rashly or make fools of themselves. Without it there is more chance of encountering an openly conceited attitude, but this will be a rarity: the truly confident do not bluster.

Still heavily balanced in front, this *M* shows vanity of a more obvious type. But unlike other pretentious stances, such as signature decorations, this vanity is not for appearance's sake, but is deeply embedded in the character. It will be wearing to live or work with. (See page 137.)

Here is a tug of war between pride and insecurity. Other people are squeezed out of the writer's thoughts and feelings, and an uneasy balance is maintained by conflicting emotional forces. All this makes for a self-centred approach, while others act merely as catalysts.

Emphasis on the second hump of the *M* shows anxiety or neurosis concerning the self. In spite of lack of confidence and self-respect the writer may be surprisingly aggressive, tilting at imagined insults or insisting on deference to himself. Calm kindliness towards him would improve the poor image of himself imprinted by parents in early childhood, and could reduce his anxious reactions.

There is a small amount of similar conflict here, but fair, steady handling without undue bolstering of confidence should produce a neurosis-free reaction. This type of minor emphasis is often temporary and may be caused by a difficult marriage.

Here is pride, emotional independence, and some irritation that other people do not appreciate how important one has been. Note the backward-facing loop, and see page 137.

This *M* shows an even, common-sense approach, with thoughtfulness for others.

Here is well controlled anxiety. In struggling not to give way to feelings which he knows are disproportionate or neurotic, this writer has created an extended upper case. This is a good example of philosophy struggling with emotion, and winning.

This writing implicitly refuses to be proud, yet there is strong awareness of the gap. The character shown in the *M* (discounting other factors in the writing) is similar to the previous one, except that this writer is trying to eradicate a feeling of superiority, rather than inferiority.

Here is a tough customer indeed, for he has converted personal pride into a philosophy, and personal weakness into accepted and unemotional fact.

This complex formation is not as self-destructive as might be feared, for the high looped stroke was created first. It shows a character trying to hide behind family achievements or family pride. The forward swing shows strong feeling, and a belief that he is creating his own destiny.

n

This calm, evenly balanced formation shows manual and mental control.

Here is excessive caution springing from animal instinct. The contracted *n* shows withdrawal from people, and other facets in the writing will probably link these two characteristics.

This painted letter shows visual concept of life. (See page 20.)

Here is a fight between the showing and the controlling of emotion. This is an exhausting form of writing flow, and it is tempting to guess an immediate emotional involvement. If it occurs frequently, and in many samples, see page 44 and page 155.

This character is easy-going, but independent emotionally. Other factors in the writing may be important. Is the *m* similar? Are there loops in *d*'s and *t*'s?

This writer is the exact opposite of the previous one. He has feelings on every subject, and desperately needs a response if only to argue with it; the emotional loops are in the thinking area.

N

N

This capital *N* is steady and controlled. Most people will find it easier to make a double first stroke, since few writers start from the base of the *N*.

Here is a painted letter, but the uprights are uneven. If such a tendency is often apparent there may be emotional disturbance. (See page 15.)

N

This backward facing loop has replaced the upright, showing a wish to return to the past, or nostalgia, since there is also an upward pull. If this formation is found in other letters refer to page 136, if not, investigate an emotional connection with *N*.

Here the *N* is slim and pulled upward into philosophical thought. Its calmness is equivalent to the classic, print-type *N* described earlier, but less practical and more inspirational.

A circle of proportionate lower case size, neatly formed, shows manual dexterity and care. If practically based it will be linked; if visually, printed.

A linked, neatly completed *o* shows discretion.

As above, this shows discretion, and the long, low-based cautionary stroke shows instinctive watchfulness.

This formation is open and honest, but careless in the upper thinking level. If it is consistent, do not tell this writer your secrets, for he may be indiscreet.

Here is excessive discretion, but emotion is sealed in too, making the writer too deeply involved in secrets to be entrusted further. See other traits in the writing: there may be disturbance.

Strong impulses are beginning to close the mind here. Motivation comes from the instinctive or physical level, and like the *a* of similar formation, this *o* is moving towards secrecy.

Here is an obsessional secret. See page 153 for possible extensions of contracted middle case writing.

This painted *o* certainly shows artistic licence, or more literally, a visual conception of life. (See page 20.)

A very tiny *o* shows manual dexterity, detailed thinking, or a wish to avoid any muddled emotional interruptions. It is often found in the writing of scholars, researchers, or skilled craftsmen.

This high-reaching formation rightly resembles a balloon floating away from earth. However, the impulse of the writer is to tie it down, since he distrusts the abstract or ethereal side of life. There will be other signs of down-pulling in the writing.

Any approximately round, full-sized capital *O* which is neatly joined shows a sense of balance and propriety.

This is a careless and rather depressed formation; its backward, concentric movement shows retrospective thinking and hopelessness. Look at other facets in the writing, since this may have been written on an odd, off day.

This may look like an extension of the previous *O* but it is quite different, since the movement is brought very positively down and forward. This shows a refusal to have dealings with the spiritual or ethereal, and an affinity with earthbound, practical things.

Here is a fast-thinking, forward flowing *O*, containing in enthusiasm and application what it lacks in self-control.

p

A closed *p* with an average length, straight downstroke shows an unusual degree of calmness and control. The downstroke must finish softly for this to be true. (See page 141.)

This is also a highly controlled formation, and the many strokes needed here show manual dexterity. In linked script this shows brain and hand working well together.

This is known as the 'dancer's' formation, showing a rhythmical, co-ordinated movement. It is often the only physical release shown in a hand of hard, abruptly ending downstrokes.

This loose, but high-pulled formation shows a yielding character who (for moral reasons) tries to please. This assessment will be modified by the downstroke ending. (See page 141.)

Here is a painted formation, with a light, detached feeling to it. Such formations may have hard endings, but this is normally unsensuous, visually stimulated writing.

Here is a very reluctant do-gooder. There is resentment in the rightward turn of the downstroke, and the measured flow of the whole shows excessive mental control. The writer should re-examine his motives. (See the similar *g* on page 77.)

This formation shows a physical state of flux. There is restlessness and wavering, and it seems that there may be a redirection of energy. (See page 148, The Lower Case.)

P

Here is a steady, balanced formation. If the right curve of the upper part extends above the rest of the writing, particularly in a signature, see page 183.

This is a dramatic formation, embodying a desire for authority as well as visual aptitude. If used in a signature refer to page 183.

This formation shows a compulsion to check facts, and to link them sensibly. In this context it is rare to have an unlinked top to the letter, and if consistent this suggests that the writer knows he has a tendency to jump to the wrong conclusion.

q

The *q* normally has a right-turned understroke, and a correctly formed, balanced and legible letter shows a desire for order and calm. N.B. If *p* and *q* are consistently reversed in mature writing see page 224.

This formation shows careless but honest indiscretion, as in the open *o* on page 105. The irritated understroke shows a dislike of being thwarted: thus this *q* shows two childish characteristics.

Here is a fast-thinking construction, and the *q* tail may also be linked. A loop in the centre case shows a sociable but emotionally involved personality. This trait should be frequently found to make such a judgement: the *q* alone is not sufficient since the writer may be emotionally involved in spelling the word correctly.

Each of the two capital *Q*'s here shows a backward-looking, slightly depressed outlook. For other *O*-like formations see the capital *O* on page 107. For the lower formation see the similar *I*, *L* and *Z*.

r

This simple formation is less controlled or considered than the following one, but shows cheerfulness.

A correctly formed *r* is difficult to join, and many writers with a sense of balance and correctness will make a break in their words at this point.

This formation is usual in other parts of the world. It is one of the few ways of joining the *r* at its base, thus avoiding introversion or 'silly ideas'. Those who use it in this country enjoy its square, practical formation.

This is basically the same stroke joined from a low-finishing letter. If it stands thus freely, it indicates a security-loving, earthbound nature.

Here is a complex character who loves his home, or possibly a past, lost home, or is strongly involved, mentally and emotionally, with his present home. There is conflict here which will make the writer seem preoccupied or obsessed.

This cheerful *r* reaches into the future and the realms of speculation or dreams. It may be part of a fanatical, upward-reaching hand, a painted letter, or an intelligent, angular idea-stream. (See page 155.)

This writer grapples with his thoughts and brings them down to a social level, probably in order to join the next letter. But a strong upward impulse is present.

This is the reverse. The writer makes a mere gesture towards the higher cases in his lower-based and linked practical hand.

Here the writer pulls backwards. If the letter is part of a back-slope this is the most natural way of writing it, but if not there is fear of the unknown here.

The small *r* is intrinsically an extrovert, forward and upward-looking letter, which is why it will (in England, where square formations are unusual) reflect antipathies to this attitude of mind. (See, however, page 136 on Victorian writing.)

R

Perfectly formed classical *R*'s are found only in the hands of those with manual dexterity, balance and control.

This formation shows wariness and control, but the loop in the upper central case shows enclosed emotion.

This painted formation is too uneven for a visually motivated person, and must count as an unfinished letter.

Here is a painted formation, its deeply plunging loop showing an emotional dimension to a visual outlook.

This is an authoritarian but caring formation. (See page 183.) Being uneven it is not a visual, but an unjoined stroke, and there may be other such formations in the writing, especially in the writing of the elderly. (See page 220.)

Here is a contrived lower case, particularly if found in a signature. (See page 181.)

This formation is a sign of self-control and independence. Even if it is found only spasmodically in the writing it shows a resistance to being dominated.

These are yielding formations, the former showing respect for early teaching, the latter friendliness and a wish to please. (A round *s* is often found in generally placid and expansive writing. See page 155.)

These formations may alternate in the writing, showing a character who sometimes asserts his independence, and sometimes yields. Note which formation tends to conclude each word. When a yielding *s* generally concludes the word, the writer usually gives in, but when the free-standing *s* finishes, the writer — meek though he may have appeared initially — invariably gets his own way.

There is emotion and a sense of form here (see Victorian writing on page 136) to which the writer ultimately yields.

This writer will not yield, nor can he get his own way: he therefore has no choice but to dig in his heels and remain neutral and immovable.

S

This free-standing capital *S* also shows an independent attitude to life, but is not as significant as its small counterpart. It can only start a word, and is thus less difficult to form.

This capital *S* shows physical and retrospective restraints. The writer may have been prevented from asserting himself in the past, and is now unable to do so. Look at his small *s* formations.

Here is retrospection become obsession. This writer constantly refers to the rules of his past life, and although he may think he is enforcing them they are in reality dominating him.

These *S*'s, which are Victorian formations, show conforming rather than yielding, with a dignified concession to correct form.

There is some conflict here between dominating past influences and ideals being realized, but the two are smoothly blended in a give-and-take formation. (See the similar *H* on page 83.)

(All t-strokes are concerned with drive)   t

The balanced *t*, with curved or straight upright, has a bar attached approximately in the middle which protrudes a letter-width outwards in a horizontal direction.

The quantity of loneliness or love-need in this looped upright makes the precise *t*-stroke seem unremarkable. This is the writing of an undemanding person who does a modest job well. Look at the other uprights carefully. (See page 144.)

This is an emphatic, slightly pedantic stroke. It may be found in any writing pattern but if part of painted script it shows thorough execution. (See page 20.)

Here is cheerful and enthusiastic drive. The *t*-stroke aims high but is tied firmly to the root of its origins, so has a logical basis.

Drooping *t*-strokes show flagging drive, and waning faith in the writer's purpose in life. Years ago one would have warned employers against this trait: nowadays it is to be expected and understood after many letters of application have been sent and wasted.

We must not make allowances for painted formations here. This writer is unreasonably depressed, for the *t*-stroke has parted from its support, and motivation no longer springs from the logic centre of the brain.

The cheerfulness of this *t* is no more reasonable than the previous one. The writer is allowing his ideas to run ahead of their logical basis.

This lagging *t*-stroke, if consistent, shows a slow comprehension. (See page 23.)

Here is a flight of fancy. The writer is indulging in idealistic or visionary projects, which are unattached to previously learned or thought-out concepts. If the whole upper case is over-developed this is fanatical writing. (See page 143.)

This *t*-stroke has been deliberately exaggerated to show a gradually thickening bar. Here is force combined with purposefulness. Anger should not be encouraged in such a writer, and other traits may reinforce this view of the writer's nature. (See page 229.)

Here is a quick, irritable temper (left) which burns out as speedily as it ignites.

All strokes which unnecessarily return to re-cross other strokes show obsessional application (right). In *t*-strokes this means double checking of facts.

This is the organizer's centrally linked *t*-stroke. The higher it is placed the more the writer is likely to be involved in the organization of ideas, and the lower, the more practical his capabilities.

Here is organization on a fundamental, common-sense or practical-instinct level.

This writer may be too busy feeling sorry for himself to remember to go back and cross his *t*. His very small loop shows that he is a controlled person: this may be temporary stress. (See page 144.)

Omitted *t* strokes or *i* dots show carelessness or forgetfulness or general lack of attention to detail.

When all the *t*-uprights are crossed with a single stroke a fast, co-ordinating brain is shown. On a high level such as this an author or philosopher is suggested, but the bar must transverse the uprights. (See page 143.)

T

This capital *T* shows a cheerful nature, though life and writing may droop as time and the writing sample progress. However, this writer is the eternal optimist and starts each sentence with fresh hope.

Here the writer draws his inspiration up from rootedly (radically) practical experience to philosophy, avoiding in a sense the logical processes between.

This is a decorated capital presented for effect. The downward-pulling serifs suggest a fear of losing touch with reality.

The straight-topped *T* shows an honest man who tries to accept life as it is. His success or otherwise is measured by his small *t*'s.

Here is emotion concerning the future (high forward loop) combined with a looking to the past for guidance. (See Victorian writing.)

This is a decorated letter. The writer is seeking a conscious effect and no emotion is involved here. Basically there are two downward holds, but they are not as strong as in the previous decorated *T*. See page 183 if it appears in a signature.

This rare *T* manages to avoid a separate top bar or loop, and can join in a forward direction. Here is a fast-thinking linker of ideas. This is an unfinished letter, and much of the writing may be illegible at first glance. (See page 22.)

u

This is a calm, well-balanced letter if joined to the following one, but the final stroke is otherwise unnecessary, indicating an earthward pull. (See page 154.)

Such a loop shows emotional involvement socially. See page 155, and the following sample below.

This formation shows even stronger emotional involvement on a social level, for loops at the commencement of a letter formation show pride and certainty; this writer is not merely reacting to his own uncertainty, as is the one above.

This is a linked *u* formation. If it is found to be free-standing the writer is making a conscious effort to lift his life from earth (practical) level and to place it among higher things. He is aware of his own tendency to be dull.

Here is a very compressed formation, demonstrating social interaction being squeezed out by ideas. This is very unlikely to be an unjoined letter, but if so see above.

When the tops of the strokes are squeezed together, secrecy is shown; the tendency to loop shows slight emotional anxiety.

This is a correctly balanced *u* in painted script, and shows a thinking character, with all parts of the brain in play.

u

This *u* can only be described as subsiding. The writing has an earthward or instinctive pull, and many other factors would have to be weighed to decide whether the refusal to rise is caused by physical bias or depression. (See page 16 and page 154.)

U

U

This is a correctly balanced painted *U* if unjoined to other letters. It shows a simple, visual attitude.

U

This capital *U* has a cautionary and joining stroke. If, in fact, it does not join the next letter but stands free, it shows a strong earthward pull, or a character rooted in practical common sense.

v

V

This is the classical unjoined *v*, showing a balanced straightforward character.

v

Here is a classically joined *v*. If however, this is not joined but free-standing, see the *u* with similar side-strokes on page 123.

The rounded *v* shows sociability and warmth, but these are at the expense of logical thought processes if the formation too closely resembles a *u*. See above regarding the side or joining strokes.

V

This very broad *v* will generally be part of an expanded hand. (See page 154.) In close, angular writing it shows a peculiar pleasure in this formation, which is a pendulum movement encompassing the whole practical brain. This is true of both the small and capital *V*.

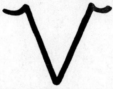

This capital *V* has wings, holding it in contact with higher planes of thought. Neither stroke is at all likely to be a joining stroke. Refer to page 183 if this is part of a signature.

w

This free-standing *w* shows a lower-based pull combined with a sociable attitude.

Here is a move towards secrecy, but it is far more marked in non-painted script. Even in expansive writing it shows a pull away from social openness.

This writer is chiefly motivated by practical ideas, but there may be other strong characteristics in the upper and lower cases.

This is a painted formation, showing an affinity towards the past. With other factors present in the writing it might show despondency or depression: it is inevitably an intelligent and sensitive formation.

W

This capital *W* (right) shows much of the brain in action simultaneously: thus it is a balanced formation. It is fact-orientated, whereas the formation on the left, with or without the inward curving sides is socially based. The tightening of the second downward curve is probably connected with the secretive aspect.

x

It is not usually possible to tell the direction in which the strokes have been made, but the formation is significant. This formation shows a balanced but factually critical writer.

This small *x* makes it clear that the writer has started at the top and returned to the top to join in. He is a man of ideas.

This socially based, but calmly formed *x* indicates a balanced, warm personality, whether it is found on joined or unjoined script.

If free-standing this shows a mentally balanced character who is nevertheless slow to move on. (See page 70.)

This sociable formation has been adapted to linking, showing a fast-thinking but socially aware personality. (See Isaac Newton's *x* on page 239.)

Here is a warm-hearted but logically careless person. (Consistent gaps in middle case letters show an incomplete logical process, often appearing in the writing of the old, but also in that of the absent-minded.)

X

This formation shows an honest, straightforward but uncompromising character.

This shows a socially aware, and probably imaginative personality, but the central joining is absent, showing a diminution in logic. Central gaps are often found in the writing of the elderly or the absent-minded.

Here is a retrospectively joined formation. A loop has been formed, and acts like a braking parachute, holding the writer to ideas of the past. This stroke may be faint and almost invisible, showing an awareness of the tendency.

y

This is a logically projected, but painted formation, showing precise and factual control.

The understroke here is severely repressed, showing unexpressed physical strength. (See page 147.)

Here is a calm, sociable and happy formation. The lower case should end softly if it is to show happy physical expression.

See above, but this is more cautious and more self-conscious. It resembles the capital *I* on page 88.

Both these formations have enlarged lower cases. They show strength which is not at present being well-channelled: physical energy which is neither being used for self-indulgence, nor willingly turned to the good of others.

For analysis of the tops see the first two *y*'s. This thinking character has weak physical impulses or little energy. (See page 147.)

Here is the sportsman's co-ordinated physical development and strength. The top shows a sociable expansion.

This *y* shows a very projected and satisfying physical life. Take note of any encroachment into other lines by the swinging understrokes. (See page 140.)

Here physical self-indulgence cuts across the central logical and social area, showing an overwhelming and sometimes uncontrolled physical need.

Here quite strong physical impulses are being controlled and channelled. If the loop is any smaller, there may be fastidiousness. Look at the pull of the writing and the size of the upper case.

Here is a gentle, fulfilled character, whose relatively small amount of physical energy or drive is spent helping others.

This character is pushing quite large amounts of energy into do-gooding, but the hard ending shows that he is not totally fulfilled physically.

Here is resentment but a seeming inability to fulfil the physical nature. Other signs in the writing may suggest a physical handicap, but this does not. There is an expansive, sociable middle case.

There is anger and frustration here, and the rest of the writing should be examined for motive. It is possible that this is a deliberately decorated letter in a very decorated hand. (See page 31.)

This is a past or present sportsman who has now dedicated his strength to communal good. This formation could be more developed. (See page 147.)

Here are frustration and anger. The writer is prevented from physical fulfilment, which would be considerable judging by the strength behind these jarred strokes.

Here there is great anger, frustration, and fear (looped second middle casestroke). This loop has narrowed an otherwise sociable formation, and it is difficult to believe that this character is happy. (See page 43.)

This character needs affection but feels consciously that others need him more. There is a strongly emotional content in the energy he expends on others. See page 155 on loops in the middle case.

These understrokes show a self-conscious unwillingness to project their (considerable) physical energy. If they appear in a signature see page 181.

Y

For these two capital formations, see the first listed small *y*. If the understroke does not project below the middle case, there is a strong upper pull, and if this occurs in a signature, see page 162.

Here is physical energy swept up into the logical area of the brain.
See above if the understroke does not extend below the middle case.
Tightly controlled lower loops may be a sign of fastidiousness.

Here is a gentle and affectionate formation, whether or not the
understroke is extended. See the small *y*'s concerning the right-
turning understroke. If this is part of a signature it shows a person
who has a role to play in helping humanity to common
understanding.

There is much conflict in this contracted upper, frustrated lower
set of strokes. The writer would appear to be torn between mental
and physical desires, and the blame is somehow due to other people.

Z

This *Z*, in the small or capital formation, will appeal to the intelligent writer who uses all parts of his brain. It transverses the whole area in a similar manner to *v*.

3

Here is a backward facing form, used by those who look to the past for their standards. (See Victorian writing on page 136.) The second of these *z*'s shows an attempt to avoid forming a lower case stroke, and this is especially significant in a signature. (See page 162.)

z

Z

This capital *Z* has a backward facing loop. Since it is not projected upwards, and indeed seems set to loop downwards, this is an attempt to form a lower case. See page 181 if it is part of a signature.

Z

See the small, similar *z* above.

This is a decorated letter formed by a brain which dislikes pure or blatant forms; it may be afraid of reality. Decorated letters are always difficult to assess. (See page 57.)

This capital formation is an enlargement of the base-line into a backward facing loop. If it extends low it is a contrived lower case, if not see below.

5. 'Victorian' Formations

The style of writing most admired in the nineteenth century eventually became known as 'copperplate', after a contemporary printing process. Many of its letter formations linger on, not perhaps in the precise format originally used, but with sufficient of its attributes to show a marked sense of Victorian values.

The following is a sample taken from a letter written by a lady who undoubtedly would have considered herself very much a lady. Note first the robust, fully developed style, with all parts and causes of the writing enjoying full expansion:

Now let us examine some of the letter formations. They are typical of the age in which the letter was written, and I am including only those which symbolize a style of writing, rather than depicting one particular character. The reader will recognize them in modern handwriting, and they are discussed as they appear in the alphabetical lists.

The upper backward-facing curve or loop.

Mrs Taylor procured

This is found in many letters, and indicates a looking to the past for inspiration and for confirmation of values. There is respect — almost veneration, for the formation occurs in the higher regions — for established codes and principles, and this is usually linked to obedience and dutiful deference to parents.

Lower middle case, backward-facing curve or loop.

the Duke of Leeds

This also shows reference to the past, and strong feelings are linked to practical purpose showing a copying of strictly taught manners (etiquette), and ways of doing things. 'Form' was all important: religion was often more a social code, as shown above, and practical matters were carried out instinctively according to the code of the 'done thing.'

Thus we find retrospective looping in the high, middle and lower middle planes of thinking. More surprisingly, perhaps, we find a strongly projected lower case:

Cambridge in January

The Victorians were far more earthy and robust than we give credit for nowadays. The Brontë sisters, who were usually in poor health, walked many miles in all weathers, and a ladies' walking map of my local area shows afternoon walks which I would consider lengthy rides. They also ate and drank to excess, and generally indulged their bodies and their feelings, bawdy and uproarious laughter alternating with the playing of musical instruments and romping parlour games.

Balanced outlet of emotion in slim upper loops.

Although there are signs of a confused blending between feelings and religion — see the tall slim loops in The Upper Case on page 144 — the copperplate style of writing allows a smooth, even but never excessive stream of emotional expression. Remember that the Victorians paid full and unashamed tribute to grief and mourning, using ritual and convention to give death an acceptable social standing. Victorian literature and drama did not circumnavigate the often sordid facts of life, and though they draped the legs of their tables it was only because there was a correct time and place for physical exposure.

Forward slope — outgoing social behaviour.

In an age of continuous discovery and invention, when Britain was approaching the zenith of her empire-building, introspection and self-discovery were not fashionable. One looked forward and ahead, did one's duty, exercised one's body in socially acceptable ways or in private, and enjoyed the dignities of self-respect and genteel emotion. Such are the values implied in my description of a letter as a 'Victorian formation'.

III
The Balance of the Personality

1. Divisions of the Personality

In Chapter I we learned to form an impression of the personality through the shape of the writing as a whole: the alphabetical lists of Chapter II took us into detailed analysis, using the emphasis of each stroke as our guide. We are now able to consider how these factors interrelate, and to realize how important it is not to make judgements in isolation.

All writing can be divided into one or more cases thus:

Upper
Central
Lower

The central case contains the largest proportion of the writing. The upper and lower cases are those which extend above and below the central body of each letter.

These three cases represent the three aspects of our personality, the central case being concerned with our mental and social approach to life, the upper case with our higher selves, including our religious or philosophical beliefs, and the lower case with our physical aptitudes and attitudes.

We must concern ourselves with the balance of these three cases, remembering Plato's similarly 'distinct classes in the soul'. He who would be 'on good terms with himself' must 'set those three principles in tune together as if they were verily three chords of a harmony, a higher and a lower and a middle.' If we find that one of the three cases appears to be poorly represented we can use our knowledge of pressure, distortions and loops to discover the cause.

For the writing to be balanced the three cases should be of equal size, and should not encroach upon one another's space:

Shall I compare thee to a
Thou art more lovely and
Rough winds do make the

However closely lined the paper, each part of the writing should have respect for the rest and allow for full movement and expansion:

Shall I compare thee to a
Thou art more lovely and more
Rough winds do make the
And summer's lease hath

Watch carefully for encroachment, and notice which case dominates:

Thou art more lovely
Rough winds do shake
And

Lower case domination.

Thou art more lovely
Rough winds do shake
And summer's lease hath

Upper case domination.

Watch also for strokes which are abruptly curtailed, but whose natural fulfilment would enlarge them grotesquely:

Warking blowing gently

Such endings show great self-control, but strong propensities. It would be interesting to look at the same hand in earlier years, to see whether there has indeed been a withdrawal of activity in that sphere. Withdrawal or suppression is always indicated by hard, abrupt stroke endings:

Washing Howing gently

Where the letter or word ends softly we may be sure that the personality is expressing itself fully without anger. Short, weak endings are the result of physical weakness, sensitivity, tiredness or impatience, but never of suppression:

Warking blowing gently

Middle case endings were discussed fully in Chapter I and in the alphabetical lists. Upper and lower stroke endings are dealt with in The Upper Case and The Lower Case which follow. Overbalancing in signatures is discussed in the chapter Signatures. See also any relevant section in The Uses of Graphology.

Exaggerated over-balancing of the personality is immediately obvious, but is not as frequently found as subtler leanings or repressions. These require a deeper understanding of graphology, but the reader should now be able to recognize them.

2. The Upper Case

All strokes which extend above the middle body of the writing come under this heading, and the higher they reach the further they stray from the influence of the tangible, the proven or the practical:

IDEALISM

RELIGION

PHILOSOPHY
IMAGINATION
LOGIC

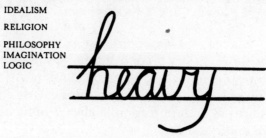

When upper strokes appear exceptionally developed or unusually short, please remember that they can only be so *in relation to the other cases*. Thus:

Over-developed upper case   Under-developed upper case

We consider upper case strokes according to these categories: unlooped, looped, bent or linked.

Unlooped strokes

The omission of all upper loops shows a thoughtful and discriminating mind, which seeks to control emotion with principle, philosophy, logic or common sense. Where the upper strokes are relatively short the controlling influence is common sense.

Hard endings (withdrawn upper strokes) show a refusal to accept a strong impulse towards religion or the esoteric.

still making

Weak upper stroke endings show a lack of interest in the higher planes of thinking. If the endings are bent see page 146.

after my life

Very tall upper strokes show a reaching towards idealism or religion. Here is the writing of a mystic.

Seventeen Thousand   died intestate

When very tall upper strokes are accompanied by unlinked *t*-bars, the brain is becoming detached from reality and parting company with all known concepts. Such writing is connected with fanaticism, and taken into consideration with other features in the writing, may show dangerous, or at least unreliable tendencies. Check the signature.

hardly thought

Upper strokes which fluctuate between high and low show a character who is constantly disillusioned or driven to act on a purely practical basis, but who never loses sight of his ideals.

settled for you

Many dedicated church people are not spiritually, but socially motivated. This is the writing of a country clergyman who has been led to his profession by compassion and altruism. Idealism is more frequently found in the writing of schoolteachers.

Looped upper strokes
Loops in handwriting are always connected with emotion, and in the upper case a balance is shown between emotion and the higher

planes of thought. The following definitions should not be applied to writing where the only visible loops are in the *d* or *t*: such writing is discussed below.

about horses

Upper loops of normal size show open affection and demonstrativeness. When they are broad, they show a reluctance to allow the spirit to soar, or a non-application of principle to emotion. If the angle of the upper strokes is variable, lack of self-control is indicated. See also the looped middle case on page 155.

don't like

Very large upper loops show possessiveness, often presented as caring.

making an effort

Very tall slim loops show much control, but there is often confusion here between principle and a feeling for what is right. (See the Victorian upper case on page 138.) In such a character manners may be synonymous with morals.

I'm taking stock

When slim upper loops are accompanied by flying, detached *t*-bars, the writer feels he has a mission, whose commands are dictated by his own feelings. It would be dangerous for such a person to occupy a position of authority.

Loops in *d* and *t* uprights
These are significant in exposing the emotion which their writer believes to be suppressed. This is particularly true when no other

upper loops, or indeed any loops at all, are in evidence in the sample.
The *d* and *t* loops act as a safety valve for people who often feel
hurt and misunderstood but either cannot, or feel they should not,
show their feelings.

the dentist

The meaning of such loops is modified by their shape, and by other
features within the writing, such as the presence of other upper
loops. All these shapes are discussed in *looped upper strokes*, and the
interpretation given applies to the *d* and *t* but with the added
emotional flavour of self-pity or resentment.

Such loops can lean backwards or forwards, or both within the
same sample, but the leaning must be in excess of the general slope
for it to be significant. See *bent upper strokes*.

Linked upper strokes

and away the   should be

When the tops of the strokes are joined and pulled down, a satirical
outlook is indicated. A light touch (light pressure — on the left)
shows compassion and an understanding of human nature, but
heavy pressure (right) linked with a low-dominated flow can be
interpreted as bitter cynicism.

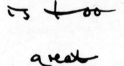

Cruel experience has made this writer bend his searching mind
into sardonic expression. There are several negative features in this
sample.

Bent upper strokes

don't like

Leftward-pulled upper strokes show regressive involvement.
Thoughts and principles are linked to the past, and parental or
school influence is often very strong.

Taylor

January

Looped upper strokes which face backwards, as described in
Victorian Formations, show emotion linked with principle. This
may sometimes express itself as misguided loyalty or sentimental
allegiance.

Lordships

Obed

Backward-bent loops in *d*'s and *t*'s show resentment towards the
past and a feeling of emotional imprisonment. This formation is
uncommon in the twentieth century, but was admired in earlier
days.

Take heart

Where the stroke turns backwards but then links on again to the
following letter an obsessional need to double-check, or to please
a past authority, is shown.

What might have

Upper strokes which bend to the right, whether looped or not, show
anxiety about the future and a mind under pressure. Look out for
other signs of mental or emotional disturbance. If the writing is
light and sensitive, this is often a sign of mental exhaustion. It may
be temporary.

3. The Lower Case

The formation of the lower case springs from the lower, or physical impulses of the brain:

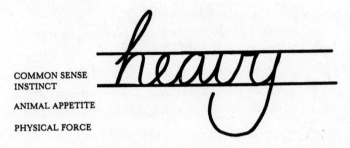

COMMON SENSE
INSTINCT

ANIMAL APPETITE

PHYSICAL FORCE

The baser or animal side of our nature is what keeps us alive upon earth. We cannot entirely deny it, and we are healthier and better adjusted human beings if we give it due consideration and expression. So strange and manifold are the effects of civilization upon physical fulfilment that for many of us the lower case remains in a state of flux. The complexities of our natures and the pull on our energies are sufficient to explain this, and it is common to find more than one lower case formation in the writing. Before imputing too much significance to this we should also remember that in our early years at school we were probably taught opposing formations. (In this print the *p*, *y* and *g* have different lower swings, while the *f* has no understroke at all.)

Nevertheless it is remarkable how frequently one of our understrokes, often the *y* or *g*, is consistently out of line with the others. It makes it very hard for us to assess the true nature of our physical impulses when we are continually confronted with apparent conflict. If many of the understrokes in your sample for analysis vary, look at the capital *G*, for the truest example of general physical bias is to be found there:

G   G   G

No understroke is required in the formation of the capital *G*, and few children create it. The voluntary inclusion of one produces a contrived lower case, and although it may be emotionally biased (an important initial), it gives an excellent insight into the writer's most honest desire for physical expression.

Fluctuation in understrokes
Because understrokes are connected with physical energy they may shrink with tiredness or illness, but they do not alter in basic inclination.

Broken or bent understrokes show physical weakness or pain in the legs. See Diagnosis of Illness.

Well-formed waverings show a minor and probably temporary state of conflict whilst the writer redirects his physical energies.

Understrokes show the usage and fulfilment of physical energy. They do not reflect conscious social attitudes. We judge a writer's physical fulfilment by the released aspect and soft endings of his understrokes. Lack of physical fulfilment is shown in hard, repressed endings or jarred, angular lower strokes. Be prepared to find a wide variation within one sample and piece together the evidence slowly. We are all more or less civilized animals, and some of us live in greater harmony with our physical nature than do others.

Looped understrokes

Looped understrokes show controlled physical energy. Here is co-ordinated strength; the writing of a sportsman, athlete or dancer.

singing mainly

There is self-knowledge, and self-control here. The writer carefully channels his physical pleasure and prevents it from engulfing other areas.

the jogging

This is the give-and-take swing. There is ample capacity for physical happiness but the initiative may need to come from other people.

always of the is keen

Here is an overemphasis on physical expression. The lower line (and upper case) makes way for the strong, deep loops. This is a sportswoman's writing.

joyful play

Here is evidence of a sensuous nature influenced by a religious upbringing. The rightward turn is more yielding than giving. See altruistic right turns on page 151.

from afar   from afar

This is a yielding, controlled formation, showing little physical pleasure. The sample on the right is similar, but with self-pity built into the central loops. See page 151 for right-turned loops.

you go

These rightward linked loops show an intense dedication towards energetic do-gooding. The writer acts compulsively, and the recipients may find such enthusiasm tiring. See page 151 for right-turned loops.

Released understrokes — physical pleasure

hardly thought

This writing shows a great capacity for self-indulgence and enjoyment. Note the soft endings, but the occasional encroachment into the middle case, when self-indulgence overrides common sense or pragmatism.

after my

These underloops cut through the mental level and try to enclose moral principle. They show a physically demanding nature, and much strength.

after a very   good day

These are well-balanced underloops, but their slightly abrupt endings show that they could extend yet further as in the above sample. Great physical enjoyment is shown.

after my life   thank you

These soft, weak understrokes show no repression or unhappiness. Upper strokes may also be weak, indicating a character who feels no agony or ecstasy, or who is temporarily tired. The latter is only true if the pressure is soft. The second sample shows a character who remains within the bounds of common-sense and logic, and may live for the present moment.

sing mainly

This is a sensitive and probably artistic (in the wider sense) formation. The writer lives mainly in the mind and spirit, although expression is blocked in the upper case. See below for right-turned understrokes.

Released understrokes — the altruistic rightward turn
Physical giving at the expense of self-gratification is shown when the understrokes or underloops turn to the right. They may be found in some letter formations and not others, showing impulses towards both types of physical release. To be genuinely altruistic they must turn willingly to the right, and not be over-controlled or held down by linking.

Washing blowing

Such altruistic turning is seldom present in the writing of young people. When found, there is probably a calling or propensity which will eventually make itself known.

after my life

Here is the true 'muscular Christian', using his physical co-ordination and strength to help those less fortunate or less gifted than himself.

making way

These are right-ward turns in the making. There is slight unwillingness to yield, but I think these strokes will continue to turn to the right, and spread throughout the writing.

plan fair

Here much good is being done for others, but physical fulfilment is being bent to mental planning, and the actual amount of expression is very small.

The unfulfilled lower case

away days   may you

These abrupt endings show severe physical repression. In the second sample an attempt is being made to bury the physical in mental activity, for the loops nudge the central case.

very good day

Here the flow is frustrated and so is the writer. He does not find physical satisfaction and is probably not a relaxed person.

very good day

This writer is as frustrated as the one above, but is trying to apply common-sense to the situation. He reluctantly gives in to others.

going away

There is rebellion, and anger, here. The writer has an unnatural or forced social conscience and should review his motives before there is a breaking-down or breaking-out from frustration.

thing is making

Physical strength plus frustration or repression equals physical anger, or violence. The pressure of the writing and the angularity of the middle case should be checked. (See page 155.)

making way

Right turned underloops which have a contracted feel about them are either in a state of flux, that is, in the process of turning from left to right, or show physical strength unable to find an outlet which pleases.

after all my

There is physical strength here, but it has been put to no special purpose. The endings are hard, showing that some form of physical activity is being repressed.

4. The Middle Case

All letters have a middle case, and many have only a middle case: accordingly we must expect its interpretation to be complex and interacting. The central area is concerned with our social selves, and reveals our motivation or basis for reaction:

LOGIC
PRAGMATISM
COMMONSENSE

Within this framework there may be tensions, withdrawals, gushings and both vertical and horizontal pulls. Released or fully expressive writing produces undistorted letter formations, but they will vary greatly according to the brain pattern or motivation of the writer.

These patterns are best divided into three main categories:

The expanded middle case : main motive : emotion

about horses

The angular middle case : main motive : ideas

try my tune

The painted or unjoined middle case : main motive : order and pattern

These categories are decided by flow, which is itself dictated by brain pattern. Within these three categories each type of writing is also subject to a vertical pull, according to the area of most influence. Thus:

Upward, spiritual or imaginative pull.

Factual pull: here all areas of the logical brain are used equally. Such writers may have underdeveloped or weak upper and lower cases, for much energy is used by their immediate mental perception. Their brain action resembles a lighthouse beam constantly circling, omitting no detail. (See page 240.)

Low-based pull, influenced by earthy or instinctive reactions. Such writers usually like to live close to nature and to animals, and become deeply attached to their homes.

Expanded middle case

Where the writing is round rather than angular, loose rather than tight, it is termed expanded. If it is carefully and correctly formed, with no incorporated loops, then it is socially orientated without undue subjective or neurotic involvement.

talking

about

When some letters are incomplete or open the attitude is strongly casual, and, depending on the evenness of the upright angles, lacking in emotional involvement. This is only true when there are no loops.

we shall

Looped expanded writing shows escaping emotion, or feelings intruding where they should not. See also the upper loops on page 143. In a socially tending hand this makes for great involvement.

Often this is the most developed of the three cases, accompanied by short upper and lower strokes. When this is so the character derives most of his joy in life from social contacts, and gains little satisfaction from solitary mental, philosophical or physical pursuits.

If the round middle case is accompanied by equally round, swinging underloops, we may expect sensuous appetites and behaviour.

The angular middle case

and sit

Where the letter formations are tight and angular, the writer is concerned with ideas rather than people; though his ideas may relate to human behaviour he himself stands aside.

it should be

Angular writing with both upper pull and enlarged upper case may be expected from an author.

the dentist

Loops in angular writing make for a difficult nature. Such a person may need from others more than he is prepared to give, but much will depend on other features in the writing, such as the *s*, the letter endings, and the capital *M* and *I*.

The whole thing

Negative features such as reversed letters, decorations or jagged understrokes make this an anti-social hand. See Diagnosis of Illness and Criminal Detection before making any judgement.

promise that

Angular writing coupled with a downward pull indicates an earthy nature. Many animal and nature lovers will have these traits in their writing, but only if it is the mòst dominant part of their personality.

The painted middle case
Strictly speaking this is an angular, unsociable writing formation, but the attitude to life is so different to that of the man of ideas that it must be discussed separately.

Painted letters indicate a visual view of life. They may incorporate strokes of many differing angles, and very often they are actually composed of circles, or half-circles. Other forms are as vertical as possible. Apart from their painted appearance they may have nothing in common.

Always for

There is much frustration and repression in this low-based, but upward soaring writing. The writer is unfulfilled and should consider putting unused talents to work.

built in the

This is a contented, earthbound person who needs others. There could be a talent for presentation or reception work.

*most
satisfactory*

This firm, capable and stylish hand still shows unfulfilled potential. The flying *t*-strokes show that the writer may realize this.

after all my

Here is gratified or fulfilled spiritual living at the expense of the physical. The writing shows sublimation rather than repression, but the heavy pressure suggests physical strength, and potential sensuality.

5. A Resumé of Analyzing Methods

We have now come to the end of basic analyzing methods, and shall soon move on to their more skilful application.

In Chapter I we examined lateral flow, or the way in which the pen moves across the paper:

Upwards or downwards
(Line slope)

Tilted forwards or backwards
(Angle of extroversion)

Smoothly or jerkily
(Conflict and distortion)

With round, angular or painted strokes
(Flow)

Strongly or lightly
(Pressure)

In this Section we have investigated vertical pull:

IDEALISM
RELIGION
PHILOSOPHY
IMAGINATION
LOGIC
PRAGMATISM
COMMON SENSE
INSTINCT
ANIMAL APPETITE
PHYSICAL FORCE

Graphology is the interpretation of the simultaneous interaction of these forces. Strangely, one of its most complex uses lies in the analysis of the most primitive of all writing samples; the earliest mark made by man, in which he etches his deepest feelings, opinions and attitudes towards himself: his signature.

I V
Signatures

1. Introduction
To make one's mark on paper is to express one's identity, and the personal information divulged by the signing of one's name is immense. Many graphology books seem to concentrate almost exclusively on this, using the autographs of famous people as illustrations, but in my experience the analysis of signatures is of more interest in connection with private, personal contacts.

Chapter V, The Uses of Graphology, will enlarge on the essential addition of signatures to any handwriting sample, and their importance in assessing strangers: here we shall set about the method of analysis.

We all use at least two distinct signatures:

(i)   *(ii)*   *(iii)*

The more signatures we employ the more we differentiate and draw bounds of familiarity amongst our fellow men. We choose our own forms of name-signing, and what we add or omit is equivalent to our style of dressing or our way of speaking to others.

(i) Betty likes to be called by her forename and is happy in that guise: her first name is written with an expansive air and an upward slope.

(ii) When she couples her forename with that of her husband's (or father's) surname, there is tension. Feel the strokes tighten, and the letters of the surname compress themselves together. Betty is not happy about her family, or perhaps about her marriage.

(iii) Nevertheless, her surname represents security to her, because
she projects it strongly in her third, chequebook signature,
and turns her own initials into a secondary cypher. She does
not think the bank will be interested in Betty, nor trust Betty's
credit.

Betty Jones has a simple, straightforward signature! Those who
feel that much has been inferred here will no doubt agree by the
conclusion of this section that she is not a complex character.

When studying signatures we must look at several of their aspects:

1. The purpose of the signature. (Page 160.)
2. The placing on the page. (Page 163.)
3. The size of the signature. (Page 169.)
4. The balance within the signature. (Page 169.)
5. Corrected signatures. (Page 172.)
6. Illegible signatures and cyphers. (Page 175.)
7. Decorations or marks of self-defence. (Page 178.)

Signatures which have been written especially for analysis are not
really suitable, as they will be stilted in flow. If no other sample
is available allow for a probable contraction and exaggeration of
self-defending marks.

2. The Purpose of the Signature

I am dealing with this first since it is important to understand the
conditions under which the signature was written. Misinterpretation
is possible more often with signatures than with any other part of
the writing and, as was discussed in Distortion, the reasons for
apparently gross characteristics can be prosaic indeed.

Try to discover any extenuating factors connected with the siting
or appearance of the signature before beginning detailed analysis.
It is important to know for whom the signature was intended, as
this will influence its size and expansiveness.

To his mother
(Expanded)

To his fiancée
(Contracted)

If you are looking at a piece of writing with a high emotional content you must expect this to be reflected, and it will not necessarily exclude financial documents!

Take note of whether the signature is to be read or merely recognized. If there is another, typed signature immediately beneath the one you are analyzing, then identification by legibility is not important, and the cypher factor can run riot.

Of the following signatures only the last two owe their formation to character rather than expediency.

T.F. Barwick

This intense pressure does not mean that Mr Barwick is necessarily sensuous or stubborn. He has been asked to press hard on the top carbon copy.

Mr Smith must countersign numbers of duplicated forms every day. It is natural that a stylized, unfatiguing cypher has developed.

Dr Carstairs has evolved a specialized and speedy signature for use on his prescription pad: the chemist will note it rather than read it. It is not his normal signature.

Much love Mary

Mary is not lacking in self-respect, nor does she necessarily dislike her name. She has simply left no room on the page for the signature.

See you soon
Ben

Ben has a wife named Bess and he tries to avoid confusion. Hard word endings are not natural to him, as a quick glance at the rest of his writing will establish.

S. Marchington

There is very little space in Sarah's family allowance book, and it is the only time she ever uses this signature.

Kit Shaw

Mr Shaw's signature is the lynch-pin of his design business. It must be attractive, unique, and easy for a machine to copy. Distortions of the writing can be caused when the name itself does not provide a basis for self-expression.

T. Evans

Tom is an athlete, but his signature contains no underloops so cannot express this. He has created an underloop in compensation.

Mary Veronica

Sister Mary Veronica's spiritual preoccupation finds little outlet in a name with few upper loops. Thus she must lift the entire signature. (This also shows a drawing away from the physical.)

We must distinguish between signatures which are to be read and those which are merely to be recognized. A busy executive has no time to make his name especially legible (it takes time to lift the pen from the page), and scarcely needs to when it is already clearly typed beneath the space left for his signature.

Very different is the letter of application, or a hand-written letter to a stranger: here the name must be spelled as well as a mark made. Anyone who fails to make his name clear under these circumstances is either deliberately throwing dust into his reader's eyes, or does not mind if he is misunderstood or his name mis-spelled.

Before analyzing a signature we should establish whether it is a name to be read or a mark to be recognized. Those who have only two signatures of similar formation are those who have only two faces to show the world. Most of us have several. But there are those, too, who choose to abandon either forename or surname altogether, and use one sole mark. Public figures or show business personalities quite frequently take advantage of the opportunity, and are known by a single name.

We seldom view ourselves as we are, and the image we project in our signatures is often the person we think we should like to be. Such an attitude is responsible for many of the strange, decorated or self-defensive signatures we encounter, but not for all. Reasons and motives for a similar response can be as diverse as the reasons for the two hundred passengers all travelling together on one particular train, and we must be careful not to oversimplify. Nevertheless, the graphologist recognizes groups and types of motive. Sometimes a signature manages to embody traits from several groups, and I am confident that by the conclusion of this chapter the reader will be aware of many of these signs, and will not confuse an illegible signature with a decorated one, or a self-projecting with a self-defending.

Very few of the following signatures are genuine. They have been stylized to show the traits clearly, as have many of the writing samples in this book. If I have unfortunately matched a real name to an admitted trait, then coincidence alone is responsible.

3. The Placing on the Page
We are taught at school, and by our parents, how and where to sign our name. Adolescence introduces forms and cards which leave no choice but to 'sign here'. Therefore to sign our name in another place can only be a rebellion or a retreat.

People who sign dutifully on the dotted line or just below the bottom line of writing are confirming to rules. We are not at present talking about the style or slope of the signature, but solely about position.

David Smith

Perfect placing shows respect for oneself and for authority.

David Smith

A signature above the line shows cheerfulness or even elation, probably connected with the document.

David Smith

A signature consistently below line level indicates depression.

David Smith

An uneven signature means that the writer is excited or anxious, or irritated by the content of the document.

David Smith

An upward sloping signature here shows confidence surplus to requirements.

David Smith

A name squashed into the left-hand half of the line shows fear, probably of authority.

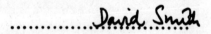

Signatures to the far right lack attentiveness and application.

...David. Smith......

A downward sloping signature shows a depressed mood rather than
a depressed nature.

David Smith

This writer wants to swamp or overwhelm a threatening
bureaucracy. It is probably his normal signature so this is really
a refusal to adapt.

until the end of that year.

David Smith

....

When the writer ignores the line and places the signature close to
the text he is showing emotional involvement with it.

until the end of that year.

David Smith

....

The writer who ignores the line and writes in the centre of the space
available is framing his name, or projecting it.

David.....Smith

The writer who fills a long line with a short name is doing the same
thing. He wants to appear more impressive than he thinks his
natural self would be.

Most of the characteristics of dotted line signatures apply to the signing of names in lists or groups, such as on legal documents or greetings cards. They soon become quite obvious to the graphologist.

David Smith
David Smith
David Smith
David   Smith

David   Smith

David Smith

The person who deliberately separates his name from the others is afraid of losing his identity, or is afraid that his importance will not be recognized:

From   Sue,   Paul,   Brian,
Penny

We are taught to sign letters below the final greeting, on the right hand side of the page, and this is indeed where most signatures are found. The characteristics of dotted line signatures still apply, but greater space available means that a further variety of abuses is possible.

Best Wishes,
Hilary

Centrally placed signatures reveal a desire to succeed and impress, but this intrinsically carries with it a fear of failure. Only by realizing this can we understand that a central signature is a move to the left, and that all moves to the left embody fear or retreat, just as moves to the right mean over-confidence and lack of respectful attention.

Yours sincerely

James Hoar

Extreme rightward placing is rash and thoughtless.

from Mary

A deliberate leftward signature shows fear of others and of failure.

Leftward signatures should be treated seriously by family and friends. The writer's behaviour will probably be odd, veering between aggression and self-pity, and if possible professional help should be sought. (See page 218, Diagnosis of Illness.) *Do not confuse with lefthand signature blocking on business letters.*

4. The Size of the Signature
The size of the signature is only important in relation to the space available, the rest of the text, and the other adjacent signatures or names.

Those with a sense of proportion and balance will normally gauge their writing to its surroundings, as was discussed in Spacing. Over-large signatures which encroach upon the accompanying text or which attempt to dwarf it have already been described as showing resistance to authority. Such writers have a need to impose their presence, although once it has been acknowledged they relax until the next (to them) challenge arises.

A signature cannot be described as large if it is the same size as the writer's normal writing.

Best Wishes

Hilary

Signature of normal size.

Yours sincerely,

Christine

Large signature.

It is interesting to compare the signature size with the size of the addressee's name:

Dear Mrs. Brown,

Yours sincerely,

Christine

Larger signature.

Darling Sylvia

Tom

Smaller signature.

If the letter has been addressed to you there will be no mistaking your prestige in your correspondent's eyes. It is possible that your name has been contracted through fear, but normally awe causes tightening without reduction in size. See Tom's signature on page 160. If you are held in affection the writing of your name will be expansive.

The size of the names written during the course of a letter is also sometimes significant: positive or negative feelings show in expansion or contraction, and this can be very marked.

Signatures which are smaller than the writer's normal script show a wish to be ignored or left in peace. This should not be confused with modesty or feelings of inferiority which may well also be present, but are not indicated by size. Many scholars, mystics or less gifted people find daily life oppressive, and would prefer to pass unnoticed. This is the true reverse side of the large signature image, where the writer wishes to project himself and be heeded.

A large signature on the left hand side of the page is far more disturbing to a graphologist than a small signature on the right.

When a proportion of the signature is smaller than the rest there is an imbalance in the attitude towards the self. This is discussed overleaf.

Those in the public eye must maintain a strong personal aura and this is usually reflected in the signature. Other writers have dwelt at great length on this topic, and I shall not do so, merely mentioning that it is fairly easy to distinguish those who enjoy the 'showman' side of their career from those who would prefer to be left to do their job, or create their works of art, in privacy.

Large signatures do not imply vanity, and I am always careful to make this clear in analyses. Someone with a large signature may be an artless extrovert, while his counterpart's shrivelled mark shows signs of pompous arrogance.

Signature size is probably most akin in meaning to writing slope, but remember that it *is always related to the surrounding text*.

5. The Balance Within the Signature
Betty Jones' relationship with her husband was discussed on page 159.

It was noted that her writing became contracted when she added her surname to her forename, but that she depended heavily on her surname (husband) when involved in financial transactions.

Imbalance in signatures is shown by a downward or upward pull in part of the signature only, or by contraction of some of the letters. Such distortions of the flow are caused by emotional connections.

James Hoare

Emotional problem regarding spouse, or, in a man's writing, very often pressure from his parents: there may be feelings of guilt or fear of failure.

Tom Evans

Tension in the Christian name suggests unhappiness or emotional unfulfilment.

Kit Shaw

When the surname is placed lower than the forenames or initials it has involved a sinking of the spirits. If the surname is larger it is respected or deferred to, but it does not give happiness.

Claire Cox

Where the forename rises happily and then plunges into the surname with contracted writing, the surname is no more than an unwanted form of identification.

Ben Roberts

The exact reverse is shown by the linking of forenames or initials

with the surname. This writer sees himself equally defined by the
component parts of his name and probably likes to be addressed
that way.

To make sure that such a joining stroke is not accidental other
signatures should be examined, besides the writer's normal prose.
Signatures often embody features which are not present anywhere
else in the writing, and may have a totally different style-or slope.
(See page 174.)

We are still talking about legible signatures, as opposed to those
which cannot be read as words. Even so, certain parts of some
signatures are easier to read than others, and this is sometimes due
to emotional imbalance.

T.F. Barwick

This writer shelters behind his surname. He feels that life goes more
smoothly for him without bringing personal relationships into it,
as opposed to Claire Cox (above) who makes all contacts personal.

When the surname dwindles away we must look at many other
factors before making an assessment.

a) Dwindling but legible, with brief or no underlining. Here is a
highly intelligent writer.

b) Dwindling and illegible, but without accompanying strokes or
flourishes. See Illegible Signatures and Cyphers, page 175.

c) Dwindling, with many enfolding strokes, loops or lines. See Marks of Self-defence later in this chapter.

When the surname is larger and briefly underlined the writer is taking pride in his family's good name. He may find it more help to him than his own achievements have been.

Here are excitement and emotional involvement, either with the accompanying text, or with whatever is on the writer's mind.

This is a complex formation and other facets of the signature should be examined carefully. Normally this is found to be a corrected signature (see below) but it may also be a dwindling one (see above), or a decorated one.

Bear in mind that the forename may be omitted whenever possible, and the surname contracted or dwindled, merely because these names are very much disliked by their owner.

6. Corrected Signatures
This section applies to all handwriting, but is especially significant in signatures, where the self is being presented.

Charles J. Drewitt

This writer, whose hand shows other signs of painstaking care, is aware that his signature is falling away, and thinks it should not, so straightens the line. The natural flow would make it a downward sloping, depressed signature.

J. Hoyle

Corrections to the signature always show deep personal dissatisfaction. These are intensified if the signature is on or towards the left. In a generally balanced and confident signature they indicate a person who is his own toughest slave-driver.

J. Smith
(J. Smith)

This rather charming attempt at self-clarification is not uncommon. Sometimes the writer achieves legibility, but often does not.

Dissatisfaction with the self is also shown in signatures which bear no resemblance to the writer's normal script. What the signature is usually striving for is a better personal image, and in this way it may resemble the decorated specimen, but this is not always the case.

Signature slope at variance with usual script

see you later.

[signature]

Here is an attempt at self-projection and panache. The writer sometimes uses this strong forward slope in his normal script, but only when he wants to impress. Questioning of many such writers has confirmed this. Few older adults have more than one style of writing, but the contradictory signatures tend to remain.

It should be

PTHawkins.

This handwriting is normally upright, though with uneven slope. The writer has emotional problems but does not want to confront them: indeed his writing shows that he has converted them into satire or even fictional imaginings. When forced into the open confrontation of signing his name, he retreats fast.

Clear script may be accompanied by an illegible signature or a cypher. (See the following section.) It may also be followed by a surprisingly ornate or decorated signature. (See page 178.) Both these variations are more common and less disturbing than the truly different signature, and the prospective employer should treat the latter with caution. See Diagnosis of Illness, and the note for employers at the conclusion of this chapter.

A concept of oneself which is at variance with one's true condition is not necessarily a bar to success, though it may prevent honest relationships. See the signatures of Elizabeth Ist and Isaac Newton in Assessing Historical Figures.

7. Illegible Signatures and Cyphers.

There are two kinds of illegible signature: that which is intended to be read and that which is merely meant to be recognized. The second category comprises all the strange hieroglyphics which pass for names, but which in reality are no more than a projection of emphasis. As such they are of interest, but should not alarm the novice graphologist who may think he is confronting every kind of distortion.

Like the totally different signature, the illegible one which is nonetheless intended to be read is far more worrying than the cypher.

There is no typed interpretation under these signatures and their writers are not known to their correspondents. We can only assume that they set very little store on a correctly addressed reply. The dwindling signature belongs to the highly intelligent 'absent-minded professor', whose mind has already moved on to other matters: the correspondent will be lucky not to receive an empty envelope!

Illegible signatures imply a lack of interest in communication. This may be denied, but the fact remains that communication is not being made. This is also true of consistently illegible script, and since the purpose of writing is communication, the writer is failing in his purpose.

None of the above applies to cyphers, which are signature-forms devised by the writer for reasons of speed, security, distinction or economy. Where a printed interpretation accompanies the cypher, the purpose of identification is fulfilled.

Sometimes cyphers are designed during the adolescent years as a kind of doodle, and are used in future years as signatures. As such they are very interesting, because the emphasis bound up in them is a guide to the potential character of the writer.

Emotion given full rein.

Emotion restricted and channelled.

Ideas linked and projected.

Physical co-ordination apparent.

Spiritual or philosophical searching.

Parental (professional) inclinations.

Sense of dramatic presentation.

Common sense.

Occasionally cyphers evolve to cater for a need which the signature itself cannot express, and this is mentioned in Decorated Signatures.

The very physically motivated person must pull his writing downwards. A name like Crane gives no scope for underloops, so a cypher is used.

Most cyphers, unless deliberately constructed along the lines of royal initials as objects of beauty, are mere packets of emphasis. The reader will have no difficulty in detecting the overriding forces in the characters of these people, and since no identification and no explanation is being given, I am including genuine examples.

Cyphers, correctly used, are fun.

8. Decorations or Marks of Self-defence

Any addition to a written name is a decoration, although the reason for its presence may be far from vanity.

The simplest decoration is a brief underlining stroke.

David Smith

The writer is saying, 'This is a deliberate signature; no mistake'.

David Smith

Two lines say, 'I hope you have noted this signature'.

David Smith

Three lines indicate a genuine fear; 'You have noted my signature, haven't you?'

These are the blunt man's decorations, or marks of self-projection or insistence. Attached to a plain signature of a similar formation to the rest of the script they are no more than affirmations of it.

David Smith

A stroke under the surname indicates confidence in the family background.

David Smith

A very long line under the entire name is literally an underlining and says, 'This is important'.

Sometimes the underlining stroke is waved or curved.

D. Matthews

This formation may have developed from straight double underlining, but in a hand otherwise devoid of all loops it has a special interest, showing a separate and approved emotional outlet, such as acting or art.

Sally Baker

This is a decoration or name frame. This is only done by those who feel they will not be noticed, and are indeed, perhaps, lost in a crowd of similar people.

Mary   *Claire*

Helen   *Jenny*

These boarding school girls will almost all lose their need for self-projection once they are away from that environment. Lines above the name show a taste for authority.

When there is no obvious need for self-projection the enlarged or decorated underline must be construed as a form of personal insecurity. We are still discussing underlines which do not touch the signature.

Fast thinkers will join the last letter of their name, or the final *t*-stroke, to the underlining stroke thus:

There is no difference in meaning between these signatures and those with a detached underlining stroke, except that these writers have more rapid brain movements. Note, though, that the underlining strokes stay well clear of the name itself.

The following after-strokes are all aggressive and seem to want to cancel out the signature.

They all show frustration and impatience with the writer's own nature or achievements, and their rising endings indicate ambition or striving.

Underlining strokes which adhere closely to the writing show self-consciousness without ambition. Some graphologists link this tendency to sexual deviation or uncertainty, but since such strokes are normally trailing and soft, and thus fulfilled, I find the above definition quite sufficient.

Tom Evans

It has been mentioned previously that sportsmen or people of physical strength and sensuousness dislike, albeit unconsciously, the lack of physical expression which a name with no under case letters produces. They very frequently compensate by creating one, as the autographs of many sporting stars show.

K Mitchell

This visually motivated character needs to pull downwards as well as up in his signature.

From Fred

This name has been altered to accommodate the lower case. It is the signature of a very young person and may change again. It may develop into a low-based cypher.

Do not confuse low-based projections or decorations with sinking or drooping signatures. (See page 220.)

Note: Low-based projections, indicating physical strength and a desire to express it, have featured occasionally throughout this book. Evidence of a contrived lower case is found in writing whose slope is normal (horizontal): individual letters or parts of words plunge steeply downwards as in the following sample:

With love

Such lower projections are often found in physically repressed writing, where hard, sawn-off endings suggest a demanding but unfulfilled physical nature. The frustration of a prolonged sedentary session or the act of writing itself could provoke this.

Centrally integrated decorations are connected with feelings. They are usually formed of loops or triangular shapes, the former relating to an outpouring of emotion (see page 155), and the latter to a highly imaginative outlook on life.

P. Celler

This writer is demonstrative and affectionate, but remember that unnecessary loops are always arms stretching out to receive love.

Many centrally based decorations can be interpreted, like cyphers, through their emphasis.

Angles in the central case show imaginative or constructive thought processes, but the angles must be forward-moving and not cutting across one another like knives.

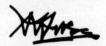

A multitude of criss-crossing angles in the central case shows hostility towards the self and others. See Diagnosis of Illness.

Valeriex

W.B.Turner

Decorations before and after the central case show a reaching out and a need to be involved in social enterprises. A trailing final letter shows a hesitancy to part or move on.

Some decorations are deliberate and indicate a character who either sets out to be, or does not mind being considered, zany or eccentric. Often this is in itself an escape from feelings of inferiority or insecurity, but not always. The rest of the writing will show the motivation: Valerie's 'X' (above) shows a happy, balanced person making an affectionate gesture.

Vera Ellis

This writing belongs to a woman who dreams rather than does. She has countless unfulfilled ambitions and likes to stand out in a crowd.

Decorations above the name usually relate to authority rather than spirituality. They should be thought of as peaked caps, showing a desire to distribute order.

Paul Kitson

This is a parental, caring and responsible letter formation. See also the 'mother-hen' *M* on page 98.

D.H.Lane

Loops which balloon over the rest of the name show affection and often possessiveness, but always vulnerability. They show a willingness to protect and take responsibility.

Signatures which show all these characteristics, but which have the appearance of being front heavy and unfinished, show a person who involves himself totally in projects but abdicates and moves on when he loses interest.

Decorations which encircle most of the name are marks of concealment or self-defence. We have already discussed the strokes which cut across the whole signature (page 180), and those which project the signature by framing it (page 165).

Some cyphers are indeed names buried in and protected by their own shell, but these will still exhibit signs of neurosis. If I ask for a further, legible signature and it is withheld, I imagine the name written in the letters of the writer's normal script, and that will usually give the answer. Such cypher-signers are wearing a mask.

This signature has been designed to hold others at arm's length. It consumes the smallest possible space, and has erected barriers. All left-sloping signatures withdraw, but those which are decorated tell you the writer's preferred role.

This role is very often parental, ennabling the writer to be dignified and secretive.

Let us conclude with a signature which would surely baffle any newcomer to graphology, but which will hold no mystery for the reader who has patiently accompanied me as far as this page:

9. A Note to Employers

I should be surprised, and a little disappointed, to hear that a candidate had been turned down on the basis of my interpretations in this section.

However, since I am presenting these analyses as facts, and am prepared to stand by them, it seems fair to say that the employer now stands warned and prepared. If, after several of his own graphological findings have proved correct, he decides to look for certain characteristics in the signature or general text, or to be deterred on the basis of others, then he will be acting on his own experience. Here are a few general warnings.

Candidates with racing, uplifted signatures may have more enthusiasm than dedication. Those who use cyphers are not exhibitionists, and may well have held responsible positions in the past: if there is no accompanying printed name, however, there may be a tendency not to take full responsibility. Candidates with clearly written, open, honest and balanced signatures may be very strong meat. After a year you may be uncertain as to who is the boss; but given respect for their strengths and talents such people make the finest supporters possible.

Applicants may exhibit in their writing those traits which you least desire in your department, in combination with those you most need. Remember that we all elicit different behaviour from those we encounter: try to discover which side you elicit during the preliminary interview.

V
The Uses of Graphology

1. Self-help — Reversing the Flow

There are known to be many physical actions which calm the mind and help to balance the character. A walk, ride or gardening refreshes the brain during a long spell of intensive study, and deep breathing has a steadying effect on an anxious mind. There are many other instances of psycho-physical effect, and graphology has a large part to play in this process.

Self-help starts with the recognition of an unwanted feature in the writing, and the wish to disassociate oneself from it. One of the most common traits in the writing of otherwise balanced characters is the loop of self-pity or emotional vulnerability:

when he went to the dentist

A conscious straightening out of the uprights will send an impulse of self-control and poise back through the wrist to the brain.

Another disliked feature, once the writer knows what it means, is the anxious *M* loop in the second hump:

Monday is the best

It will take about two months of positive alertness and effort to banish the loop, and there will probably be an intermediate stage when there is a break and a re-starting in the letter formation:

Monday is the best

The writer will find that the omitting of loops which are *not in appropriate places*, that is, those in *d*'s, *t*'s and the central case, has a dignifying effect upon the brain. But to abolish loops where they have a natural place is a repressing action, and will probably force them to re-appear in another place. It is not a sensible thing to do:

I don't want any loops

It happens quite frequently without any reference to graphology, however. If a writer decides that his handwriting is childish or too relaxed, he may exercise strong and undesirable control over his personality by restricting the flow. The reasons for the change of style are not good ones, and what was once a natural, gradually maturing hand has become the repressed markings of a tightly reined-back personality:

over at Framlingham   over at Framlingham

So, we must consider carefully before deciding to reverse the flow. We must be sure that what we want to change is a weakness or imbalance, and not an inherent part of our nature which we should instead recognize and accept.

We may not like the untidiness or wild strokes in our writing, but if we are fast-thinking or imaginative that is how it will appear. Think carefully before attempting to change something which is positive. Negative features have been delineated clearly during this book. On the whole they are small individual strokes coinciding with a small facet of our nature, but occasionally they are massive distortions. Even here surprising results can be achieved: it is not possible to feel really aggressive when you are making loops. Those with very angular or criss-crossed writing may care to try.

after my life

Trying to extend the upper or lower cases where the endings are already soft and apparently fulfilled may prove difficult and frustrating.

Where they are obviously repressed it should be a rewarding experience:

anyone   *anyone*

The feeling of well-being is the proof of a worthwhile experiment. Here are some negative features which may be eradicated to very good effect:

m m   m m

Conceit or anxiety.

T   t

Loss of contact with reality.

t   t

Brain ahead of actions.

into   *into*

Absent-mindedness.

very   *very*

Very angular middle case.

above   *above*

Unfinished middle case.

got   *got*

Over indulgent lower case.

get   *get*

Unwilling altruism.

get   *get*

Physical repression (not so successful).

John   *John*

Decorated signature (you will soon stop feeling naked).

been   *been*

Stubborn endings.

Most of these features are due either to minor anxieties or carelessness.

If you really feel you are not sufficiently independent or do not project yourself well, it might be helpful to try the following formations:

S

Independent *s*.

M m

Uninvolved capital *M*.

y

Forward understroke.
(Difficult if the impulse
is not there.)

d t

Controlled *d* and *t*.

Reversing the flow is at its best when controlling *excessive* looping, thus helping to foster self-control and purposefulness.

2. Understanding Teenagers

It is sometimes difficult to interpret the behaviour of young people from their actions or comments. For reasons often based on their own unhappy experiences with parents or teachers, they may think that to reveal their true feelings will be to risk ridicule or punishment.

Many teenage problems are due to unfortunate personality combinations at home. Children are not able to choose their co-habitees, and usually have very little chance of parting from them. An extroverted child in a generally introverted family may appear to be the odd man out, and may question or dislike his own character; still more so the introverted child in a generally extroverted family. Similar clashes are likely to occur at school, and it is possible that one unsympathetic teacher could blight a personality and a future.

Mental disorders requiring trained psychiatric help are fortunately rare amongst young people under twenty years old, and the use of graphology with teenagers can be very gratifying. They can probably be helped best by consistently positive attitudes: once they have learned to recognize their own strengths, they may easily notice and appreciate the different gifts of their friends and families, and may come to feel safe in asking for help with their difficulties.

This section is really for teenagers themselves. I took an independent interest in graphology at the age of twelve, and although my study had as then no name, it taught me a great deal about tendencies and potential. I hope that young people will make their own assessments, as I did, and that parents and teachers, and all who have contact with teenagers, will open their own minds to the possible benefit and support afforded by analysis.

As was discussed in Distortion, checks should be made on messy or illegible writing to make sure that short-sightedness, physical illness or an unsuitable writing position is not responsible. Boredom or fear may turn writing into a chore, but more practical causes often lie behind straggling or uneven script.

Changes also featured in Chapter I, and at no time are they more frequent or more welcome than during schooldays. However, it is not at all the same to write differently over a period of days or weeks as to produce two different styles within one sample. John and Peter are brothers aged sixteen and fourteen:

The statute   *The statute*

John's writing is quite different in slope from last week, and it may be different again next week. This is not a matter for concern at his age, since slope relates to his social attitudes and these are yet to be fully formed. The important thing is that the slope is consistent within the sample. *perpendicular style*

Peter's writing has a variable slope in the uprights, showing slight emotional disturbance, but it is the strained and uneven joining pattern in his script which may be responsible for its constant changes in appearance. He seems to be trying to link his script and to tilt it forward, whilst the natural flow of his writing is upright and unjoined — painted. We do not know why Peter feels he must control his pen in this way, but the result does not look easy or happy, and something is worrying him enough to cause the uneven uprights.

The first aid treatment for anxiety is often genuine praise. We can certainly praise Peter for his skill in attending to details (close *i* dots) and his structured, self-reliant way of doing things (firm, upright formations, independent *s*, and neatly crossed *t*).

We can ask Peter what sort of writing he admires, because very often a strained or stilted style comes from an attempt at copying the appearance of a parent's (or hero's) writing. In fact, the changes in both John's and Peter's letter slope may be connected with their father's character:

standards must be maintained

Father is an impressive person, and his writing shows qualities of leadership and tenacity. There is self-control in the ironing-out of loops in the *d* uprights, showing an emotional nature carefully channelled but not repressed. It is not surprising that both Peter and John admire and subconsciously emulate him. However, the wholeness and beauty of an individual's nature is his alone, and both John and Peter have many admirable facets in their writing: they will grow up to be themselves, and do not need to model their characters on anyone else.

Sometimes strong and positive qualities are the very ones the individual is trying to submerge or deny. Let us stay with painted formations a little longer, since they are often a source of unnecessary anxiety instead of (as in the case of Elizabeth 1st!) immense pride.

visual

Many sensitive, artistic or visually gifted young people find it hard to accept their disinclination to join up letters. Although there is less pressure nowadays to conform, there are still some people who think that writing is only mature or correct if it flows in linked script. The whole personality may relax if the writer realizes that the impulses of his brain are dictating the right pattern for him, and that his pattern carries particular abilities.

However, he may consider altering it if the stroke endings are hard, showing repression or frustration, as in this sample:

do my prep.

Dissatisfaction with one's writing shows dissatisfaction with one's character, and in the teenage years this is rarely justified. Constant amending of the letter forms (without a change in the slope) often indicates severe self-criticism, or destructive comments from teachers, parents or friends.

enjoying myself

Christopher finds his plain, abrupt downstrokes disturbing, so adds serifs to them. The result may please him visually but it has not solved the problem, which may have its roots in his unfulfilled physical nature. Without discussing his writing at all he should be encouraged to explore and relish new sporting or energy-consuming activities, and to enjoy as many physical pleasures as possible — which could include eating, laughing, handling animals or just having a bath — until he finds one which suits his nature. Such fulfilment would probably banish self-consciousness, and in time the letter endings would gradually soften and the serifs disappear.

Christopher's frustration may already be connected with sport. Many schools make this an area of intense competition rather than enjoyment, and whilst encouraging young people to do their best it is implied that their best is never good enough. Those who are sensitive or feel that they must be capable of better performance may suffer considerably under such a regime. It is worth invest-igating the teenager's attitude to sport whenever the underloops are sawn off or distorted. Sexual problems will produce similar signs of physical frustration, but will usually be accompanied by emotional disturbance (variable uprights), superfluous upper loops and uneven line slope and word spacing.

Whilst very young children feel that they are 'wrong' and all adults 'right', this is not the case in the late school years. The teenage problems discussed up to now have been largely due to over-sensitivity, and are not basically personality problems at all, but questions of self-acceptance. Mary, for instance, thinks she is a social failure:

My name is Mary. I am 15 years old.

Any reader who has studied the earlier sections will see that she is sensitive (light pressure), yielding and eager to please (curled *s* and soft endings), well-controlled (almost all loops omitted), but truly not drawn to intimate contacts with most of those she meets (upright slope and wide spaces between the words). The anxiety shown in the *I* and *M* is probably due to criticism from others.

Mary's writing suggests that she might be very gentle, and good with small children or old people. But, like Peter, she is reserved. She is not gregarious and cannot cope easily with the playground jungle. Although she may always find it hard to adjust to large numbers of near neighbours, she has an affectionate nature and should not be allowed to feel inadequate. The slight back-slope and the large gaps between her words show that she may shed her anxiety if she comes to see herself as a quiet person, happiest in small intimate groups.

Signs of emotional disturbance and anxiety may indicate conflict with parents or at school. This conflict can be avoided when it is realized that the impossible is being asked of a child.

every evening

Mark's massive physical energy (heavy underloops) dominates his life, and even if this is only true for one month it should be respected. He is not likely to want to sit quietly, and rebellion must be expected if he is forced to do so for long periods.

services in Calin

Paul's behaviour probably matches his listless writing. Note the light pressure, downward slope and unfinished letters. Extra sleep and good food should restore his drive and purposefulness. If they have failed to after after some weeks, then causes for depression should be discussed, and counselling considered.

Remember that the signs for tiredness and demoralization are the same in handwriting: drooping lines and *t*-strokes, loops in the *d* and *t*, and bowed upper letters, especially the personal *I*. It is surprising how seldom the tiredness factor is tackled first, for although it may be subconscious or denied, the treatment for debility is simple and can often save the psychological probing which many teenagers find so embarrassing. The concern which goes with quasi-nursing may be welcome too, since laziness can spring from the feeling that, 'No-one really notices what I do'.

Where there is no sign of distortion, conflict or excessive self-projection the teenager should be encouraged to respect himself as he is, and to have his gifts or positive attributes pointed out. (The list of writing features at the end of this chapter may help.) He may enjoy making his own bias pattern, too; this is described in Choosing a Career. Sadly, the comments we make to young people are all too often totally negative. It is probably quite natural that a sudden burst of self-assertion may antagonize parents and teachers, neighbours and friends, but a knowledge of graphology can help both in finding the reason for self-assertion and in understanding it.

Many so-called problems arise from unused talent. Much of graphology's power lies in the detection of *tendency and potential*, and the teenage years may be the most satisfying of all in which to put it to work.

change trains

Pat's writing shows that she is strong mentally and physically. The pressure, forward force and linking, together with a capable *t*-stroke, controlled loops and both an interest in people and a desire to please (*i* dot and *s*), show that she may need a challenge, such as a social project or the Duke of Edinburgh's Award Scheme.

more temperate

William is quiet and sensitive (light writing), but his tied *t*-strokes show him to be an organizer of ideas. He needs scope for this.

try my tune

Sarah's joined *t*-strokes combined with deep pressure and upright, spaced out wording, show that she has much energy for projects. She may work best alone, but can be trusted with overall organization.

The war of the Roses.

Susan's high uprights show her advanced philosophical development, and the *s*'s indicate self-sufficiency. This is intelligent writing (easy, encompassing flow) suggesting that she might benefit from stimulating educational surroundings and older company.

Most people   *for the week*

Both Christine and Ruth are unhappy, as will be immediately obvious. The patterns in the writing are complex and disturbed, but whilst Christine's problems concern the present, Ruth's light writing and backward-looped *f* look to the past for help. Both fear the future, and both need a great deal of reassurance and love. They may find it beneficial to take their anxieties outside the family or school circle, and talk to someone who is uninvolved, experienced and sympathetic.

Note: These samples were checked for accidental distortion, and all signatures carefully analyzed.

befent the castle

Distortion is marked in Ted's reversed letters and filled-in *e*'s. His
need for other people (words close together), and two yielding
formations (*f* and *s*), combine with the regressed or omitted *t*-strokes
to suggest someone who may be younger in social development
than his actual years. He is not considered dyslexic since there is
no word-inversion in his writing, nor does he have undue difficulty
with spelling. If his actions give himself or others cause for worry,
an outside counsellor may be welcome.

Generally speaking, graphology is best practised by teenagers
themselves. When they are treating it as yet another study or interest
they will probably view themselves — and their friends, parents
and teachers — quite objectively, and will learn analyzing skills
relatively quickly. When they are undergoing stress it is usually
desirable that they themselves should assess the problem, though
warm but uncritical support may be acceptable. Cynics may say
that the practice of psychotherapy amounts to no more than the
gradual acceptance of unpalatable home truths. Youth, quite
rightly, looks to the future to bring fresh situations and a dispersal
of former shadows, and will tend towards the converse view; that
the purpose of any kind of psychoanalysis is to foster self-respect.

Young people also appreciate that graphology is a new science,
but they find it an exact one. They are inclined to be less assertive
than many adults when starting to analyze, and more ready to learn
slowly. The guidelines of conventional fact absorption and step-
by-step teaching methods prompt them to assimilate one stage before
moving on to the next. There should be many excellent graphologists
amongst the next generation, and I hope they will retain their
optimistic view that people can, and do, create their own destinies.

The following ideas for drawing out latent talents can be applied
at any time of life, but I have included them here since this is the
age when new paths are generally picked. They are a simplified
but cheerful list of graphological traits, preceeding the more detailed
study of bias patterns explained in Choosing a Career.

painstaking i dot

Good attention to detail.

cautionary strokes

Will not act rashly.

Light pressure

Sensitivity. Once this is seen as an asset the personality will probably flourish, often showing imaginative talent.

connected t stroke

Organizing ability.

not joined up

Visual ability; a sense of balance, order or presentation.

Tiny careful letters

Craft skill. The pen is being manoeuvred intricately.

Round writing

Affection. This person could care for younger children.

s stands solo

Self-sufficiency: works well alone.

tied t stroke

Reliability. This person will see a job through.

high dotting

Interest and involvement in other people.

giving g's

The altruistic *g* shows a desire to put energy and effort into helping others.

above the line

Optimism. A cheerful person to have around.

closed o and a

Discretion. Will respect confidences.

closed esses

Submission. Makes a good helpmate or employee.

flicked i's

Flicked or joined *i* dots show a sense of humour.

Decorated script

Decorated script is a self-projection. Encourage acting, modelling or demonstrating. (See decorated signatures.) She wants the limelight, so let her try it.

3. Choosing a Career
Career officers or school careers teachers place stress on aptitude

and ability when advising young people. Unfortunately greater difficulties lie ahead for them than ever before: they must be slightly over-qualified academically for what they want to pursue, and must then project themselves outstandingly during an interview. Even when they are fortunate enough to be selected for further education, and diligent enough to gain their specialized qualification, they must prepare themselves for a further stint of self-justification and self-projection.

It is unlikely that their parents suffered to quite the same extent, though their grandparents may well have done. Choosing a career nowadays could more aptly be called, 'Finding paid employment'. Graphology can assist in this gloomy situation in two ways; firstly by finding positive qualities in the writing, and secondly through the analysis of bias patterns, as shown later. Let us look first at X, a young man who achieved his ambition with much hard work but very little misery. Since we are not at present discussing aptitudes but *personal qualities*, his new career need not be specified.

living in Edinburgh is

1. His working brain is unfettered by social, emotional or neurotic pressures. (The loops are in the right places, the middle case is neither expanded nor contracted, and there is no undue emphasis on the second downstroke.)

     This is, of course, to some extent a matter of luck, but parents and teachers can help a young person to be able to deal swiftly with threatening problems whilst he is still a young teenager, as the last section indicated. He will then know himself sufficiently well to recognize situations which may be difficult for him, as they arise. X is not immune to emotional pressures, nor is he an unsociable person, but his sense of balance has not allowed him to permit intrusions into his working status. His weakness might have been his tendency to involve himself in other projects, but he knew this, and rationed his activities.

2. His physical needs have not been neglected. The underloops
    are structured and controlled, but have good depth and normal
    pressure:

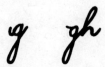

3. The higher planes of thinking, philosophy or religion are
    absorbed by his working brain. Note that one happy or balanced
    stroke links all three cases, allowing each its full expression:

4. There are signs of independence without aggression or fear:

    These will allow X to make decisions without questioning them
    afterwards and without fear of reprisals. His decisions are made
    by a well-integrated brain and are not likely to be very contro-
    versial ones, though the strongly linked script suggests that they
    may be self-centred:

5. X likes, and is curious about, other people. The consistently
    highly placed *i* dots show that he is far from being totally
    engrossed in his studies and indeed at times must detach himself
    resolutely from others.

6. He is prepared, in spite of his independent nature, to listen to others and to keep an open mind:

in Edinburgh

This is shown in the reasonable (two letter width) gaps between the words, and the soft upturning to most of the word endings.

Superman? X does not think so. He thinks his writing is childish, and wonders when it is going to become more mature.

There are several lessons to be learned from X's small writing sample, and they are not greatly concerned with aptitude or intelligence. The numbered points above are considerations of priority within a balanced life style. X is actually eager to achieve much within his present working sphere: more simply put, he is ambitious. His signature stands clear and unvarnished some distance from the rest of his correspondence, which means not only that he wishes to be selected, but is sure that he will be. It is often possible to cultivate qualities such as those described above by flow-reversal, or deliberate training of the writing as shown in Self-help — Reversing the Flow; but it is naturally rare to find so many positive qualities in one sample, and the average so-called achiever will probably find no more than two or three.

Bias patterns

All writing, however, contains a bias pattern, and we make use of it in considering *aptitude*. Graphologists recognize that there is a certain bias of flow in each individual's writing, pulling it upwards or downwards. This was explained in The Balance of the Personality, and it is not easy to understand the formation and meaning of bias patterns without first having reach Chapter III, and become well acquainted with the functions of the upper, lower and middle cases. An understanding of repression in the upper and lower cases is necessary, because sometimes a potentially dominant case is actually absent!

In a sense, bias patterns are a graphologist's first impressions. But just as the ear of a mechanic would have to be very experienced to diagnose car engine trouble precisely, and the eye of a doctor would need to observe the entry of many patients to his surgery before he felt able to hazard a guess on sight, so it is necessary for this analytical skill to be left until late in the book. It cannot exist in isolation, and detailed knowledge of stroke formation must lie behind its practice.

Making bias patterns for other people is advanced graphology, but it can be surprisingly easy and rewarding for the individual to make his own.

1. The first stage in making the pattern is to look at the writing and assess its vertical pull, or balance:

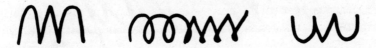

| Upward (Philosophy, idealism) | Centrally encompassing (Social or cerebral) | Downward (Practical, physical) |

2. We then decide whether it is basically rounded, angular or painted in formation:

| Rounded (no points) | Angular (pointed *a*, *n*, etc.) | Painted (unjoined) |

3.   We must now choose the weakest or least emphasized case; the case which has no strong pull towards it, and we must, *for the purpose only of finding aptitudes*, discard it. We neither look for, nor hope to find, unbalanced writing, but in assessing aptitudes the slightest domination in one case or the other is important. For example:

IDEALISM

RELIGION

PHILOSOPHY

IMAGINATION

LOGIC

PRAGMATISM

COMMON SENSE

INSTINCT

ANIMAL APPETITE

PHYSICAL FORCE

1. Upward pull.   2. Angular writing.   3. Lower case weakest.

The bias pattern of the writing above will appear thus:

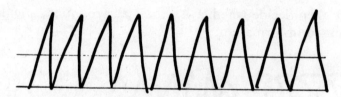

When selecting or discarding cases, allowance should be made for repression, as the following sample shows:

your cheque   your cheque

Expressed personality   Potential personality

Bias pattern of the writing above, allowing for full expression of the personality.

The sample above has been assessed as rounded, since that is the general appearance of the much larger sample it was taken from. The bias patterns on the following pages are described individually in terms of aptitude. The reader will know if the occupations suggested are beyond his intellectual powers, but *it is the environment and atmosphere which are usually all-important.*

round writing   shows social motivation.

angular writing   denotes the man of ideas.

Painted letters   indicate a need for pattern and order.

Bias patterns combine the motivations of each individual into a visual shape. Each shape suggests a different type of occupation, or a different environment, and these are listed under the patterns.

A few detailed definitions of vertical pull may be helpful before the bias patterns are studied:

An interest in philosophy or religion.		Upper pull (may be linked to central case).
Vivid imagination.		Flow in top middle case.
Strongly factual bias.		Mainly central flow.
Common sense motivation.		Flow along base of middle case.
Instinctive or intuitive drive.		Flow very low, often balancing an imaginative flow.
Practical or physical skill.		Lower pull, linked to middle case.
Physical co-ordination.		Long slim loops, often encroaching.

Strong links may be found between two of these forces.

Rounded bias patterns

(A)

This is sociable writing, and the writer is suited to working with people as long as the gaps between words are not large. Isolation or limited company may not make for happiness, unless the pressure is very light. (Office work connected with the general public.)

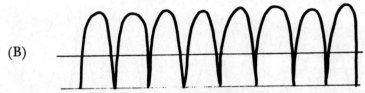

(B)

Sociable formation. All the thinking aspects are linked to higher planes, though the upper area is contained and controlled. The writer is suited to any caring profession, but is not strongly practical. (Social work, medicine, law, teaching, etc.)

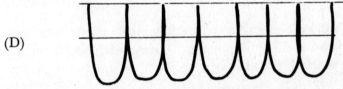

(C)

Here common sense anchors a strong spiritual pull. (Church ministry, mission work, medicine, nursing, etc.)

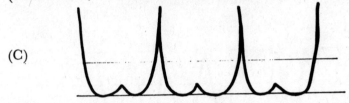

(D)

Here is a writer who will apply friendliness, thought and common sense to a practical job. Look for signs of manual skill in the writing, or love of animals and outdoor life. (Physical or manual work, farming, sport, practical skills, land management or work with animals, etc.)

Angular bias patterns

(A)

Here is a combination of practical thought processes which, as with X, stop short of imagination and instinct. This is the scholar's penetrating mind process, and may also be found in round or painted writing. However, in angular writing the concentration tends to be more exclusively cerebral. X, by the way, is a solicitor. (Business, law, factual problems, research, logistics, etc.)

(B)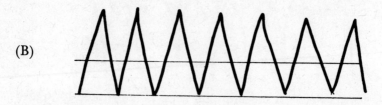

Here thoughts and ideas are linked with the inspirational. (Researcher in arts subjects, historian, publisher, journalist, reformer, librarian, book-shop assistant, etc.)

(C)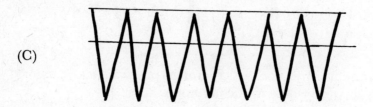

The writer will probably be engrossed by his thoughts and ideas, but may enjoy travelling or moving about out of doors. (Practical science, research, accountant, archaeologist, travel writer, experimental farmer, etc.)

(D)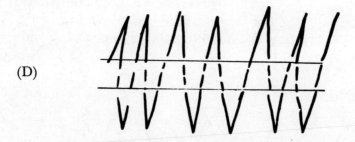

This pattern does not linger in the middle case, but consistently joins the inspirational with the physical. The writer may have to choose between (B) and (C) above, but may also have a unique contribution to make in giving to others, for he can translate the unworldly to the worldly. Much depends on other facets of the writing. (Dancer, missionary, kibbutz worker, social worker in deprived areas, morally motivated sportsman, etc.)

(E) All encompassing flow.

This enthusiastic writer may find it necessary to link all types of brain activity together. He may not be able to sit still in an office, and may need equal freedom for his thoughts to take flight. (Estate agent, salesman, politician, travelling work, etc.)

(F)

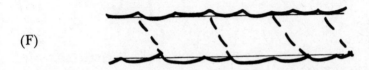

This writer links the imaginative with the instinctive, and has intuitive aptitude. His strongest thought processes are metaphysical. (Journalism, psychology, advertising, writing, satire, composing, astrology, etc.)

Painted bias patterns

(A)

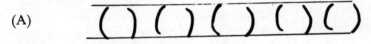

A practical but essentially cerebral visual nature. (Art work, demonstrating, presentation or reception work, special visual skills, etc.)

(B)

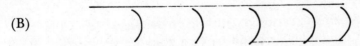

This is very sensitive writing. The writer may be unsuited to working amid large numbers of people and might be happier involved in a special skill. (Any engrossing subject where he will be allowed freedom of expression without constant social contact.)

(C)

Here is a visual encompassment of the logical, practical and physical. There is a need to complete and perfect according to a design. (Engineer, surgeon, dentist, conservationist, architect, surveyor, inventor, instrument maker, etc.)

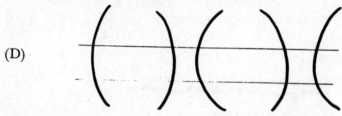

(D)

This pattern is relatively rare and shows well-projected skills. It is a fulfilled formation and is not likely to be found in a young hand, but if it is, the writer should 'follow his star'. (Entertainer, performer, preacher, musician, public figure, etc.) If the writer does not identify himself with this interpretation, he may be happier returning to the pattern (A) on page 209.

I feel, with some despondency that these bias pattern lists are inadequate. It is obviously impossible to cover every subtle blend of emphasis, which is why the method of pattern-making has been simplified; but I have included the most frequently found patterns, feeling that an inability to help everyone is a poor excuse for helping nobody.

4. Marriage Guidance

There are two ways of looking at this subject, and either way my title is inaccurate.

No one is going to cancel a wedding on the basis of my analysis, nor marry a man whose brain pattern I advise as suitable. Nor are they going to remain married to a man they dislike because of what I say, though they may find it a good excuse to divorce him. Sadly, graphology is not effective as a guide in one in a thousand marriages.

The second way of looking at the application of graphology to marriage tends to furnish both partners with sticks for beating one another:

'Look at your bossy *t*-strokes.'

'Well, you seem to get your own way just the same, judging by your final *s*'s.'

Neither application amounts to anything very positive, and could cause marriage problems which did not exist earlier. So, we are going to have to abandon both guidance and marriage, and look instead at people; at individuals. Let us forget our partners, our imaginary knights in shining armour or the women of our dreams, and luxuriate in looking at ourselves. Having progressed so far with the study of graphology the reader must by now have some idea of the balance and bias of his own personality. If he has not scrutinised his own handwriting, or has actually opened the book at this page first, he will now have to find a sample for analysis.

In Understanding Teenagers it was suggested that graphology could be of great help because the personality had not had time to become grossly repressed or distorted. On this basis, the reader should, if possible, find a sample of his own adolescent writing. If this proves impossible he should produce the earliest sample he can above that age. Two samples are even better, if taken from two different ages. We shall now use an example to show the purpose of the study. Here is Christine, married for fourteen years:

Aged 11 years:

'I was very happy at school. I had lots of friends and was at the top of the class. But I was not happy at home.'

Aged 15 years:

Christine Moore

'I was not so bright, but was still very sociable and still not happy at home.'

Aged 20 years:

in creasingly for

this theatre

Much research

'I hated college life though I loved my subject and was good at it. I had lots of boyfriends, was infatuated with one who wasn't interested in me, and I was still a virgin.'

Aged 25 years:

Branch

Officers Married

Quarters

'I adored my first baby though he never stopped crying. I had married the chap I was in love with: sex was super but we had some terrible rows, even then.'

Aged 32 years:

take her place in his

affections, specially

since for the first

time that through

'We had fun, especially with the children, but I went through a terrible depression and felt suicidal. About this time I seemed to stop needing friends. Sex was O.K. but rarely earth-shattering: we still had terrible rows.'

Aged 38 years:

But to what purpose

Disturbing the dust

I do not know

'Nothing much has changed except that I don't feel suicidal any more. I have masses of acquaintances but no real friends, though I could if I wanted to.'

Chris's main feeling now is that she has failed somewhere. We are going to use graphology to discover what has happened to her personality, and this is the pattern for the reader to follow. The chapter on Changes is important here, but if the whole book has been well assimilated, analysis should not be difficult. Chris's signature has hardly changed at all in pattern. There is a tightening in her forename and a plunge downwards into the surname: but the surname is expanded. The reader should analyze changes in his own signature, using the chapter Signatures.

Notice that we are not concerning ourselves with Chris's husband.

We are concentrating on Chris herself, the changes in her character and the needs of her character. The pattern of her marriage makes no sense to her and, even using graphology, it is necessary to go much further back than marriage for it to make sense.

Aged 11:

I walk

gh deaths

This is the youngest possible age for analysis, but it is interesting. The writing is not really very happy, or fulfilled, but features of Chris's character are already marked. The self-accepting I, organizer's linked *t*-stroke, and strong attempt at independence shown by the free *s* still survive. There is humour in the *i* dots (not shown), and extensive letter linking showing drive. The words are sociably spaced, but the slope is upright or backward (variable) and the writing is basically angular. The upper case is repressed.

Aged 15:

Christine

Moore

This is only a small sample but the change in sociability and need of others is great. On the other hand the drive is lessened, and there is more caution and yielding. The *M* is still free of fear, and a sense of humour is again present. The upper case is developing, showing an interest in philosophical or religious matters.

Aged 20:

in creasingly

Much research

theatre

This is strong writing, mentally and physically. The upper case is slightly repressed, but imaginative mental processes draw strength from it. There is much physical expression and activity, and a strong self-centred drive. Note the balanced *M*, organizer's *t*-stroke and retained sense of humour in the *i* dots.

Aged 25:

Branch

Officers Married

The writing has diminished. It has above all lost physical strength and confidence. Note the signs of social anxiety in the *M* and *d*, and stilted attempts at enlarging the upper case. The humour is increasingly satirical.

Aged 32:

affections ept

since for the

Physical strength is further diminished, and the pressure is very uneven, showing an ebb and flow in strength which is in rhythm with some project in Chris's life. There is a little emotional disturbance and self-irritation in the corrected letters. There is more lack of outside interest than further diminishing in confidence, but far greater distance between words showing a holding of others at arm's length. The upper case is very variable. The brain is still very active.

Aged 38:

Disturbing the

The writing is still emotionally disturbed and the angle of extroversion is now markedly pulled back. The lack of physical strength, or tiredness, is now prominent; even the *t*-strokes are losing their strong drive. The brain is still very active but there is a conscious downward pull on the upper case. The *s*'s have a defeated look about them, suggesting an unwillingness to yield but an inability to be independent. The whole balance of the personality is unsettled, as though there is only so much energy to be distributed, and Chris cannot decide how it should be allocated.

Such is the history of Chris's personality in terms of graphology. We are still not going to consider her husband, since for all his part in Chris's personality he could be dead, divorced, imprisoned, abroad or sitting by her side while we talk. We are staying with Chris and her personal attempt at fulfilment.

The main driving force of her character, portrayed in her bias pattern (see page 209) is two-fold, and runs through the imaginative-thinking (upper) and the instinctive-thinking (lower) strata:

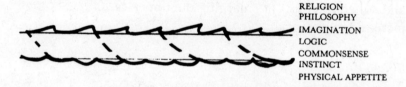

RELIGION
PHILOSOPHY
IMAGINATION
LOGIC
COMMONSENSE
INSTINCT
PHYSICAL APPETITE

Her intuitive vitality encompasses her whole personality, but there is possibly a weaker link in the middle of the practical brain. All her life she has been the type to be strongly and enthusiastically involved in projects, and the instinctive sensuality of her nature, added to a sense of humour (and a sense of the ridiculous), have helped her to derive enormous pleasure from them. What she clearly did not bargain for, and still seems not to have realized, is the vast pressure which a marriage and children put on a personality which cannot do anything by halves.

In taking pains to see that anything her family tackles is properly organized and supported, she does not have much social energy left, and in fact sees any other social contact but fun as a further infringement on her project time. Of course, if something fires her imagination or her instincts it has to be included in the schedule, so she is almost always physically tired. Her suicidal feelings were based on escaping from pressure. Her nature does not allow her to do things badly, and she is perpetually 'in harness'. It is quite probable that any normal family would make use of this characteristic, thus pushing her further into simultaneous frenzy and exhaustion. When she was a student she was able to concentrate on her own imaginative and instinctive projects only, and they were obviously sufficient to fill her life entirely by themselves.

So, we come to the purpose of this investigation, which was to establish Chris's weaknesses and Chris's needs; or *your* weaknesses and *your* needs. Chris's weakness has already been established. Her first need is to accept the nature of her weakness, and her second need is for others to accept her nature as it is, and to say to her from time to time, 'This is very bad for you, being who and what you are'. This is the reverse of the usual pattern which results in the individual saying that he or she is not 'understood'. The spouse is rare who can understand a partner who does not understand himself! Graphology sets the pattern clearly before our eyes. Even if Chris could change her husband she would still be left with her children. She must establish her needs, and ask for them to be respected. Let us look again at her bias pattern:

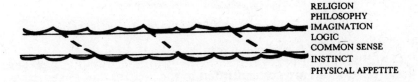

RELIGION
PHILOSOPHY
IMAGINATION
LOGIC
COMMON SENSE
INSTINCT
PHYSICAL APPETITE

There are gaps. Chris needs those close to her to apply brakes in the form of philosophy and practical common sense, and she needs physical help and brain rest (sleep and relaxation). She needs affection and appreciation — who does not? — and she also needs freedom to pursue those projects which philosophy and instinct have helped her to decide are priorities.

She also needs her strengths to be needed, and this is where the two partners can help one another. It is quite possible that Chris's gifts of imaginative thought-linking and powerful instinct have been confused by herself and by others, and taken for energy and capability. Now that she knows they are not that, she can tell others so. Should Chris have had the good fortune to be drawn by instinct to a partner who naturally supplied her personality gaps, she might not now be so tired, but there is much hope and room for improvement.

Assessment of character balance starts in the teenage years, and graphology can help to prevent unbalanced relationships from developing if the adolescent is made aware of his own needs, and his right to seek for them. Those who disapprove of introverted speculation may retain closed minds if they wish, but they and their children will be the losers. The search for a perfect partner will continue, being one of mankind's undiminished yearnings. Graphology's part lies in first finding the self.

5. Diagnosis of Illness

I am fully aware, and have always been aware, that by involving himself in this field of study the graphologist is stepping on dangerous ground. If, however, he regards himself as no more than a metal detector, unable to dig anything out and making no assertions or promises, he will do no harm and may prevent unpleasant situations from developing further.

Turning first to signs of physical illness, we remember the sample of grossly handicapped writing:

Next Christmas Day

Here disabilities are concentrated in the central and lower cases, representing those parts of the body. Motor action is retarded, but there is no mental disability. Physical handicap produces a jarring but weakened movement, quite different to that involved in mental disturbance. The reader will be sufficiently acquainted with flow to realize the confined nature of this interruption:

visit my sister

This suggests that the writer has hip or knee pain. If any reader is dubious about such interpretation I suggest he examines the writing of someone whom he knows to suffer from a defined physical handicap. He will find the weakness marked in an appropriate part of the writing.

Pain in the trunk of the body is indicated in the central case of the writing. Here is a painful arm, shoulder or forearm:

Shortly afterwards they

Weakness in the inner body is indicated by frequent faintness in the central case:

next year they

Headaches or migraine, and often mental pressure as discussed later, are shown in bowed upper case writing:

What might have been

Before making such an analysis check that there is no external reason, such as an uneven writing surface or jolting movement, why there should be interruption in the flow.

Uneven pressure may be due to weakness or pain, but you must first be sure that a poor pen, emotional excitement or some other accidental, external reason is not causing the ebb and flow. Weakness or pain in the legs will naturally hamper physical expression, but a person may suffer in this way and still retain much lower case expression if he enjoys eating, laughing or sex:

go away on Friday

Tiredness and depression have been discussed earlier, and it was noted that both are indicated in handwriting by downward-dropping line-slope. Physical exhaustion will often result in a writing pattern which is indistinguishable from depression, not only in the line-slope but in the drooping *t*-strokes:

only three more times

Such writing may also be accompanied by a lifting or decrease in pressure. Tired writing should not be confused with unfinished writing, which shows a quick, active brain but impatience:

three more times   *three more tim*

Tired writing.   Unfinished writing.

Demoralization caused by tiredness, ill-health or trauma is quite distinct from endogenous depression caused by mental conflict or malfunction. It is easily recognizable by the above signs, whereas depression in more complex disorders will not be so easy to isolate.

A diminished capital or personal *I* is a sign both of physical exhaustion and of mental depression and reduced self-respect. If the depression is due to tiredness, this feature will be short-lived:

I went   *I am not*

A small signature, however, is merely a sign that the writer wishes to be left in peace. Other signature formations are discussed on page 222.

No graphologist, however amateur, is likely to confuse physical illness with mental illness, for in physical illness the flow is interrupted, not distorted. For this reason it will be clearly seen that physical deterioration of the brain consists in weakened or jarred strokes, that is, in gaps in the flow from the brain rather than in flow distortion. Here is the writing of an elderly person who has

no mental disturbance at all: lack of *t*-strokes and *i*-dots shows
absent-mindedness at any age:

It. Axelby (Sister)

(H. Axelby [Sister])

Nor is the graphologist going to be in any doubt about emotional
disturbance, which has been much discussed already:

about that time

Unparallel uprights indicate emotional disturbance. There is no
mental illness here.

Mental illness begins to show itself in the appearance of gross
conflict within the writing. When there are disturbed, bizarre
impulses of the brain, or a loss of contact with reality, the
graphologist sees or feels the disturbance and recognizes that the
writer is largely beyond his power to help.

Certain patterns in grossly disturbed or distorted writing occur
sufficiently frequently to be diagnosed as connected with anti-social
behaviour. See Criminal Detection. Other patterns, full of loops,
are seen to be extensions of emotional disturbance:

when she said I was

Loss of touch with reality is indicated when upper bars and strokes
are detached from the supporting upright stroke. However, neither
this nor the excessive looping above is likely to be found in isolation
— indeed, they may be interconnected — and the writing as a whole
will show gross disturbance:

I'm eatingstone

Self-hatred is apparent in 'cancelled', leftward positioned or downward-sloping signatures.

(Cancelled)   (Leftward)   (Downward-
                                             sloping)

This may be allied to over-correction of letter formations, but it may also be connected with anti-social features. The graphologist should be wary of commenting on such traits, remembering that if the writer points this out and asks for help this is occasionally possible (see page 186), but he is more likely to deny the features or hide the writing. Be very careful.

Decorated signatures (see page 178) are less likely to be caused by severe mental disturbance than those which are totally different in style, slope, size or pressure from the rest of the writing sample. Such deliberately different signatures are not usually disturbed in themselves, but like free-floating upper bars, show a lack of contact with reality:

The signature (bottom of facing page) shows wishful thinking, a desire to be more flamboyant and sociable than the writer feels she is, but the writing itself shows no disturbance, unlike the sample below:

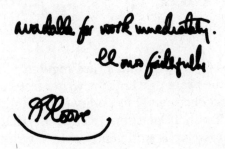

It is often the balance, or lack of it, between the signature and the rest of the script, which indicates the writer's conception of himself. A sudden change in signature style may be deliberate, and caused by dissatisfaction with the appearance of the writing: this in itself shows dissatisfaction with the self.

Sudden changes in the signatures of adolescents are to be expected and up to a point, welcomed. After that age it is unlikely that the signature format will change without other changes in the writing becoming noticeable. (See Understanding Teenagers.) Accordingly, the graphologist should regard signatures which are altered in isolation as the first stages of cyphers (see pages 175-7). Signatures which change in relationship with sudden developments or omissions in the writing as a whole indicate a personality change. Such changes may be associated with signs of secrecy:

This writing shows mental pressure in the upper case strokes and contraction in the social area, as well as the inked-in *e*'s and *a*'s of secrecy. At present these do not amount to mental illness, but they are sudden changes and will be affecting the personality adversely. If more negative signs appear in the writing it will begin to have the disturbed look which warns the graphologist that he is encountering a malfunction of the brain.

Other sudden changes which are a cause for anxiety during, but particularly after the teenage years, are inverted letters:

I bont delewe in   pruickly

(I don't believe in)   (quickly)

When the *d* and *b*, or the *p* and *q*, are regularly interchanged, a malfunction of the brain prevents the writer from understanding, or making, moral decisions. His ability to tell right from wrong is impaired. See Criminal Detection. (Remember that no child below the age of about twelve is sufficiently able to write automatically for this to be of concern, and where there have always been mechanical writing difficulties this age can be extended.) We are concerned with mature adults, and with sudden changes.

Graphologists cannot treat personality disorders or malfunctions of the brain. When they encounter inversion it is sensible to suggest that the writer try to differentiate between *d* and *b* in his writing: the problem (including possible dyslexia) may be discussed, and the writer's own assessment of it may lead him to seek help. In fact, it is likely that anti-social behaviour will soon place him in professional care. Major conflict or brain disruption is shown by criss-crossing strokes in the middle case, and the onset of this can be alarming when it occurs in a well-known hand:

I wait until you come

Since the middle case is concerned with all practical thinking, muddled or anti-social ideas will soon be apparent.

Sometimes intensely angular writing will begin to develop signs of compulsive thinking, and this will have the result of a criss-crossed appearance similar to the sample above. Remember that obsessional double-checking is shown by a return to, and a re-crossing of strokes already formed:

Here today, gone tomorrow

Other forms of compulsion are shown by a refusal to join letters except in one direction, which naturally gives the writing a strange appearance:

over to my mother

Such writing denotes compulsive behaviour, which may be confined to small repetitive acts but which may also lead to offences such as that described on page 227.

The section on emphasis mentioned the rare upward emphasis to be found in some writing. It is not easy to detect, but will be found in conjunction with other signs of fanaticism, and is another indication of compulsion:

I'm Taking stock

The features discussed during the last few pages are signs of disintegration. The character has become dominated by a brain impulse which threatens the balance of the whole. Grossly distorted, mentally disturbed writing will probably seldom come the novice graphologist's way: but if he should encounter such signs, or the merest onset of them, in the writing of those he knows most intimately, he is then in a position to suggest constructive help, instead of suffering fear or anxiety.

Psychiatrists, clinical psychologists and those who study the psychology of medical illness or medical conditions, constantly research new methods of diagnosing, comforting and healing. My hope is that the speciality of graphology will one day be adopted by someone already grounded in such practice.

6. Criminal Detection
The graphologist has long been given credit for his work in the fields of identification and definition of motive, but much experience is needed before he can undertake vital police work. The following crimes and samples have been altered to avoid recognition, but each

depicts a certain type of criminal motive. Over-simplification is probably necessary in a graphology book for beginners, since marks and indications in the writing are often subtle and diffuse. We can, perhaps, learn from these cases where we ourselves could be weak and vulnerable: they are divided into the following categories:

1. The action of the compulsive, deluded or mentally disturbed.
2. The intelligently planned, deliberate forgery or embezzlement.
3. The strongly physical or violent crime.
4. The once-in-a-lifetime misdemeanour.
5. The wilful 'kicks' of the authority-hater.
6. The foolish actions of the socially inadequate.

1. The Action of the Compulsive, Deluded or Mentally Disturbed

The previous section will have shown the reader how a malfunction of the brain can produce an imbalance in the personality. All its emphasis and drive seem to be concentrated in one area of thought. The following miscreant sold military secrets, thinking that he was God's agent on earth, sent to hold the balance of power in his hands:

The signs of his compulsion could have been detected several years earlier by anyone who has read this book, for they would have noticed the upward emphasis, obsessional back-joining strokes, and the upper loss of contact with reality.

The following writer was eventually convicted of theft from those she worked for in the guise of a home help:

Her writing tells us that her personality badly needed to give and receive affection. When the affection was not given to her in sufficient quantities — and it could never have been, since she was craving for her own mother who had left her as a child — she 'stole' it in the form of possessions, usually worthless ones. A graphologist would have seen her neurosis, particularly in the *M*, *d* and *t*, slowly develop into such a hunger that she felt what she took to be her right. Note the compulsive backward-looking loops: a tendency to join in one direction only was mentioned in Diagnosis of Illness.

Our final mentally disturbed criminal is a psychopath. He has a poorly developed sense of right or wrong, and to him want and need are synonymous. He removes anything which obstructs his path, and there is sadly little hope that he will ever be welcome in society.

(I saw your dog fighting)

Notice the absence of emotional disturbance, the poised personal *I*, the smoothly intelligent flow and the lack of repression in the understrokes. Only the constant inversion and strong, self-willed linking give signs of his condition.

2. The Intelligently Planned, Deliberate Forgery or Embezzlement

The following writer used his financial acumen to make illicit deals. He remained undetected until his obliquely boastful comments alerted a friend, who had noted the writer's inappropriately high standard of living. Pride was this writer's downfall, and apart from an apparent ability to handle money, and some signs of secrecy, there is little else in the writing to suggest imbalance:

As the motive of this crime suggests, intelligence in the practical middle case is likely to be a strong feature of any embezzler's writing. This, however, is no sign of a crook; nor indeed is there any sign of deceit in the writing above. Secrecy, yes, but this is relatively common in the middle-aged. There would be no real grounds for investigation if it were not for the writer's signature:

Firstly, the cypher is noticeable in having a distinctly frightened backward pull, which is steadied part-way through, but never achieves the forward flow of his normal script. More significantly, the cypher ends in a clearly inverted *d*; the writer's name ends with the letter *d*, not *b*. This formation is either a sub-conscious disguise or a literal mirror image of his honest self.

The next embezzler, on the other hand, has immediately disturbing signs in his writing, and should have been suspected sooner than he was:

The middle case shows profuse but strained thought involvement, with literal double-crossing in some of the letters. The *t*-strokes are anxious or obsessional, and secrecy is strongly indicated. Note, too, the alternate tightening and expanding word formations, indicating that a smooth social manner will have been largely maintained. Caution is strongly shown before each word but 'Easter', where the capital *E* rises from the level of the other letters, showing excitement. This *E* is described on page 71 as demonstrating an unusual balance between logic and instinct.

Instinct is responsible for this criminal's activities, for motivation arises from the lower thinking brain. There is some mental disturbance here, but I doubt if it would prove strong enough to allow diminished responsibility. The yielding *s*'s suggest a meek character endowed with low cunning. (Note the *h*.)

We had better include a female forger, but this woman truly belongs in the once-in-a-lifetime category:

for Monday week

Mental strain, secrecy and lack of self-respect show in her writing: for six months she drew her sister's pension during her absence in Australia.

3. The Strongly Physical or Violent Crime

The following writer has had strong anti-social tendencies for a long time, and is full of hate. Easily roused to anger as a young man (with a violent background), he had suppressed his tendency to lash out physically for several years. Whilst taking part in a robbery he was confronted by a store manager who resembled his father, and though the rest of the gang ran off, he stayed to beat up the manager, who later died.

after we done my bike

(after we done my bike)

There is a downward pull in the writing which is abruptly halted or repressed, giving a strongly physical nature no outlet. Emotional and social disturbance combine with fear of people (looped *m*) and a capacity for sustained anger (widening *t*-stroke). The very angular, upright, unsociable writing is twice corrected, showing irritation at the self, and the lack of cautionary strokes shows impulsive action. This writing tells of a tragedy, for there is no mental illness, and this man could have been helped to channel and express his physical violence. It is a story of unresolved childhood fear and aggression.

The second violent crime was committed by a very different character, but under fairly similar circumstances. The writer was a retiring, scholarly man, but given to fits of impotent rage which he dared not express in public or even to his family, though his study occasionally bore marks of them. Pressure built up in him until he strangled the cat after it had made a mess in his study. He did not admit to this, and when his wife tried to make him do so, he strangled her.

Pools of ink mark the unfulfilled and unfinished strokes in this totally repressed writing. Not only is the lower, physical case cut off, but the upper and middle cases are also deprived of expression. This is not a true painted formation, and its natural joining pattern, though depressed and downward-sloping might have been a form of character projection and acted as a safety valve:

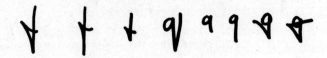

Patterns of violence may show in the writing of many people who do not commit crimes. There is no question that jagged understrokes, particularly when they are tightened and compressed as well as bent or shortened, show repressed physical anger or frustration. Such strokes should be noted and discouraged:

See page 186 in Self-help — Reversing the Flow.

4. The Once-in-a-lifetime Misdemeanour
The mother defending her young is probably the most obvious and understandable instance of a crime blindly and almost innocently committed. Nevertheless, only a certain type of character would risk manslaughter as did Mrs S.

Driving her two young children home from their play-group in central London, she was alerted to the fact that one of them was about to make a puddle on the back seat of her new car. She took a short cut through a bus lane, and was flagged down by a policeman. Unable to convince him of the direness of the situation, or to stop him talking, she rolled him over the bonnet of her car and drove on: ten minutes later her home was surrounded by anti-terrorist police. The policeman was unharmed, and the charges against her were eventually reduced to dangerous driving, for which she received a two-year driving ban.

sending you the next installment

Mrs S's writing shows her to be highly developed in all parts of the personality, though with a tendency to distance herself from others and strong self-will. She is probably a gifted person who has been successful and received deference, but this time neither charm nor an articulate presence had achieved anything for her. The severe curbing of her precious liberty imposed by the ban will undoubtedly be enough to prevent her ever appearing in court again. Note the total lack of all dishonest features, and the high expectancy that others will share her idealistic views, shown in the soaring upper case. Both these characteristics will often be found in the writing of those who do wrong on grounds of principle.

5. The Wilful 'Kicks' of the Authority-hater

The first of these characters is a miscreant on grounds of principle. He is young, and no mental illness shows in his writing, but unless he is helped now to come to terms with the need for authority, obsessional tendencies may develop. He has been fined twice for resisting arrest whilst taking part in a demonstration of protest, and subsequently served one month in prison for intruding as an unauthorized person on government property:

mark is coming on sunday

The lack of capitals, tradition-defying *i* dots, and slight neurosis about the future shown in the upper *d*-stroke do not amount to mental disturbance, but the writer is unlikely to grow out of these feelings of resentment without psychotherapy.

The second writer is a police-hater, and specializes in anonymous letters to her local station, to a hospital consultant and to the housing officer: she is not a criminal but has been bound over:

I have grounds for complaint

The heavy, slightly obsessional (certainly double-checking) writing has a strongly defended and secretive personal *I*. There is a relentless self-projected drive in the flow, and the writer is confident about her next action, for there are no cautionary strokes. The very unusual underhook on the *p* would soon identify her.

6. The Foolish Actions of the Socially Inadequate
Lack of intelligence, a sheep-like desire to be acceptable in his circle, and true financial or physical deprivation combine to produce this unfortunate thief. He has been known to break and enter for the sake of finding and eating food, and to leave afterwards with a few articles under his coat, but without his pipe. He does not mind his frequent prison sentences since they are a natural part of the pattern of his life:

15 storey buildings

His writing shows a low mental age and a retarded brain (trailing *t*-strokes and cautionary strokes on free-standing letters). The uneven height of the letters indicates anxiety over the process of writing.

7. Assessing Historical Figures
A personal encounter with a celebrity long since dead is an intriguing experience. The graphologist is able to investigate in depth and at length the traits which made each figure great, and to wonder at the inevitable human weakness so carefully channelled and controlled. A visit to a museum becomes a session of lively interest rather than a perusal of dead objects, for the greenest graphologist will make more vital acquaintance with the great than the most learned of his neighbours who does not know how to look at handwriting.

Though limited here to nine famous characters, I have tried to encompass many interests. Since virtue alone puts little handwriting behind glass, greatness must consist in achievement: accordingly we expect to find strength of purpose, self-projection and signs of infinite attention in these brief analyses. Yet the compelling force behind the achievements of these artists, scholars, statesmen and soldiers is almost invariably unexpected. Many signatures are at odds with their accompanying text, showing limited self-knowledge, and self-projection generally gives way to absorbed dedication to a vision or project. Irritation with physical weakness or need is shown by frequent upper case encroachment: there is a tendency amongst achievers, it seems, to close the mind to unwanted intrusion or distraction.

For each extract shown, many documents and letters were studied, so that judgements which may seem to have scanty foundation are actually based on the analysis of several samples. I am grateful to the staff of the Students' Room at the British Museum for their patient help.

Albrecht Dürer (1471-1528) *Drawing and notes, 1508*
Subtle tendencies are swept aside here by an unusual and irresistible bias pattern which swings relentlessly from side to side like a pendulum:

This lateral movement, allied to engraving, is frustrated in the writing by mental and physical pressure. There seems to be a weakness in the lower left limb, inhibiting Dürer's rare, harmonious figure-of-eight swing (often found in his notes as a quill-testing doddle). Note the catch in the cypher *D*, and the flinching lower left case throughout the writing. Exasperation with physical achievement is shown in the cancelling of the lower strokes by the upper case of the following line, and these problems of strength and impulse are echoed in the eager but weak *t*-strokes, variable slope in the upper strokes, and erratic lower case. Pressure is light,* showing

*Throughout this chapter the photo-copy appearance of pressure is deceptive.

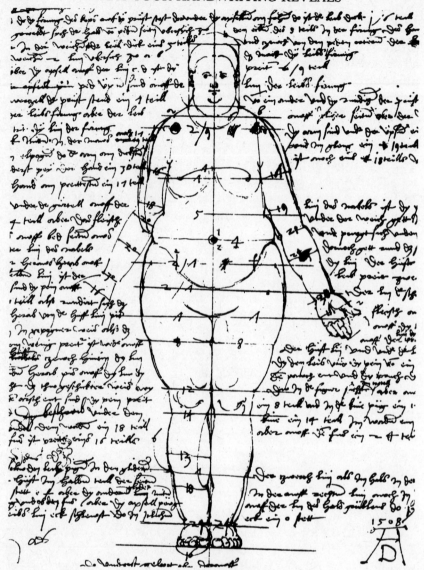

Albrecht Dürer

sensitivity, and the artist clearly drove himself hard — note the many self-corrections — never lowering his standards nor ceasing his search for perfect form. Though the writing is reasonably close-set, indicating a need for others, the angular formation and precise *i*-dots combine with the revealing but role-stating cypher to exclude social demands on himself.

The cypher expresses a wish to be seen as a pioneer, yet the protective 'house' implies weariness, a desire for stability, and above all a need for surrounding family to be kept in their place and allow him unhindered artistic development. Visually cerebral searching dominates the writing, dwarfing social, physical, emotional or philosophical pleasures.

Elizabeth I (1533-1603) *Letter to James VI of Scotland, 1588*
The 'skribling' admitted to here is a conscious abandoning of style, for every page of Elizabeth's writing begins with a line of neatly

Elizabeth I

painted script and swiftly disintegrates into flamboyant illegibility.
But the splendid lightening flash stroke with its implicit portrayal
of boredom and irritation is anchored by a low-based, intuitive pull:

There is no abandoning of attention in this complex script, but
a constant pull between self-will and self-preservation. Though the
s's never yield, the *A* and *t*'s show a tormented double-checking
of facts and details, and the watchdog of retrospective awareness
is always on guard: even the deliberately enigmatic personal *I* seems
to glance over its shoulder. The upper strokes are high-pulled and
often encroaching — though occasionally bent or jarred showing
mental pressure — but the lack of loops and the channelled or
restricted lower case show inhibited physical and emotional
expression, which the signature interprets.

Astonishingly unchanged since the unhappy days before
accession, Elizabeth's signature indicates emotional release through
lavish, stylized ritual and etiquette amounting to drama. (See page
179.) It shows a concept of herself from which the Queen refuses
to deflect. She invests tendency in role, deeming the histrionic
gestures of her position safer than spontaneous emotional
expression: thus her instinctive sense of self-preservation combines
with a need for total fulfilment in an impenetrable pageant, relished
equally by monarch and state.

Galileo Galilei (1564-1642) *Letter referring to telescope improvement, 1609*
Galileo's inventive talent springs from the central cerebral area,
and his flowing script is often linked by the *t*-stroke (organization
of ideas). Encroachment shows intolerance of his own physical
appetites or failings, and the writing, despite its potentially strong
upper case — note its almost fanatically detached high loops as they
alternate with harshly repressed uprights — communicates mainly
through logic:

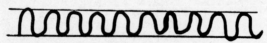

Dominant though such a bias may be, emotion and grievance are also integral features: disruption in the line slope, resentment in *d* and *t* loops, and anxiety in the *M* combine with altruistic and parental signs to suggest that his good intentions are often misunderstood. A great need for others is shown in the close word spacing and fairly rounded writing, and the discreet *a*'s and *o*'s show meticulous social attention.

That his inventions must be noticed and approved is shown by

Galileo Galilei

the distancing of the signature — more so on other documents — and that they are not, causes distress. (Galileo was tried by the Inquisition for heresy.) Honesty and integrity shine from this writing, but the many disruptions show less ability to separate himself from the social world than most outstanding scientists. Middle case contraction may indicate pain in the writing arm, but the locking loops on the final *m*'s suggest psycho-physical tension. Italian temperament or no, Galileo's achievements were not always accompanied by personal happiness.

Oliver Cromwell (1599-1658) *Letter to his cousin, 1643* (*opposite*) Though the calm, elegant signature apparently tells all, this desperate and emotional letter indicates severe inroads into the writer's self-confidence. Cromwell is a man of both instinctive and intuitive vision (linking and emphasis at base and top of the middle case), and there is a deliberate withdrawal from the very high or very low planes:

The nature of Cromwell's vision is complex, but it seems that his faith lies in the practical rather than in the imaginative. As he pleads for money to fund his New Army, his own physical needs, never great, are repressed and controlled, and the upper case is held down or filled with morally inspired emotion. (See page 138.) The word 'God' is twice corrected in agitation, as is the *M*, showing faltering faith in God and self. The line slope becomes increasingly erratic, and the letter uprights variable. The wide word spacing and angular formation, in conjunction with precise *i*-dots and a contracted forename, suggest projected ideas rather than social involvement, and the soft final *s*'s a yielding to expediency. (Low-based or omitted *t*-strokes seem to have been a feature of seventeenth century handwriting, and backward-turned *d* uprights, showing tribal deference, remained fashionable until the Industrial Revolution.)

Only in the frantic post-script do the gaps between words narrow: here emotional involvement all but eradicates the aloof, controlled independence which the signature and personal *I* suggest is Cromwell's conception of himself.

Oliver Cromwell

Isaac Newton (1642-1727) *Notes on Gravity, 1769*
and message to Mr Dillon, 1714
Here is pure, intense cerebral power with little to detract from it.
In the earlier writing manual dexterity combines with close concentration, and in old age neither senility nor infirmity mar the
script. The even, encompassing flow (see page 154) has such middle

case bias that in excitement it merely becomes neater and tighter, as if trying to disappear inside itself:

The writing is rich in cautionary strokes, and the frequent patches of wet ink suggest vividly the rapid, precise pen movements and

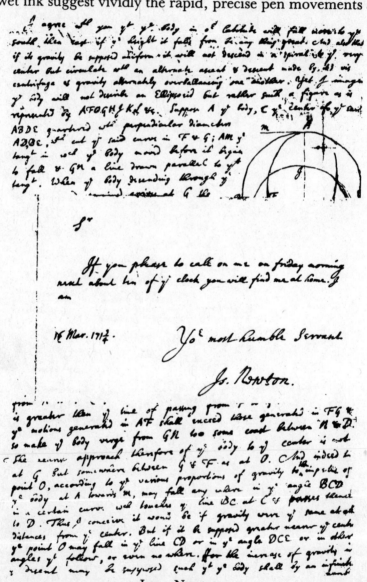

Isaac Newton

stabbing quill-dipping as the flow from brain and pen imprints itself in meticulously formed order. (Note the unbroken *x* and perfect legibility of 1714.)

Honesty, discretion and moderation (*e*, *o* and *M*) are its highlights, and a balanced, easy flow its general tone. There is no encroachment of cases and emotion is expressed naturally via the loops in *b*, *l* and *h*, yet we note the intransigent *s*, the stilted altruistic turn, the wide word spacing and top-closed *W*, the elation and self-absorption as the theory expands satisfactorily . . . and perhaps the extraordinary signature does not come as the anachronism it at first appears. Here, in letters four times the size of the text, Newton stands revealed; Newton stripped of his calling, nakedly self-centred (strong linking, large signature), fussy (*t*), formal, and lacking in moral focus (distorted *e* and *w*). Science alone can balance and fulfil this character.

George Washington (1732-1799) *Letter to the Earl of Buchan, 1793*
Concentrating as always on bias and motive, the graphologist finds in George Washington a weary but loving guardian angel.

The bias pattern has a broad, arched flow with strong upward emphasis:

There is a distrustful attitude towards physical pleasures — note the uplifted *G* of the signature and the tense lower case strokes — though the writer has great self-knowledge and generally gives that side of his character sufficient room for fulfilment. The signature shows signs of a determined upward pull and physical cramping, and the two contrived centre case loops in it show nostalgia and regret. Both signature and text show a character eternally aware of the potential snares of the flesh, and the uplifting, crowning signature decorations amount to a feeling of divine appointment.

Fatherly dignity and caring rest in the controlled upper case letters and overhanging *W* and *h*'s. The generally tired but enthusiastic *t*-strokes have both upper zest and at times pragmatic organizing power. The clear *e*'s and *a*'s show a man of integrity, and the soft *s*'s a yielding to expediency and authority, the latter originally being parents and their values (retrospective upper loops). His own self-esteem is high, as shown in the front-heavy *M*, and the writing generally shows the qualities of a patriarch. The close word formation indicates a liking for the company of others, and the unusually round and released writing, affectionate and caring motivation. Idealism bound to a gregariously loving nature denotes a social reformer who practises what he preaches.

George Washington

Horatio Nelson (1758-1805) *Letters to Lady Hamilton, 1803 and 1805*
We must say at once that Nelson has written with his left hand for
eight years, having formerly been right-handed. In spite of pain,
frustration and diffusion of energy, the sociable writing of this very
human hero has a physical bias:

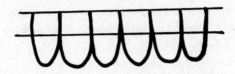

Be ever my Dearest Emma your
most faithful attached and
affectionate
            Nelson & Bronte

Battle, may heaven bless you prays
your Nelson & Bronte octᵗ 20ᵗʰ in the
morning we were close to the mouth of the
Straights but the Wind had not come far
enough to the Westward to allow the Combined
fleets to Weather the Shoals of Trafalgar but
they were counted as far as forty Sail of Ship
of War which I suppose to be 34 of the Line

Horatio Nelson

Disregarding slope, which may have suffered an enforced change, the writing seems constant in its small tendencies, small conflicts. The upper case veers in faith or disillusionment from high to low or down-held, but disillusionment does not quite deter altruism, nor does the need to yield (bent or soft *s*) destroy self-respect (proud and caring *M*). Frustration is absorbed into the next action (*f*), and pragmatic lower joining frequently extends to the *I*, showing great personal involvement in projects. Duty and respect for past authority are shown in the *b*'s and *f*'s, but there is a strong contraction and pulling away from the left which could be contempt for mindless etiquette, or simply the constant pain which since 1793 was intermittently 'as if a girth were buckled taut over my breast.' Note especially the *d*'s above the signature.

Variable drive and irritability (weak or sharp *t*-strokes), secrecy and indiscretion (blind *e*, open *a* and *o*), each have a place within a kindly framework. These are long-standing facets, as are frustration (jagged *f*), occasional obsessiveness (backward-linked *t*), and pronounced humour (comma-like *i* dots). Nelson's signature — very seldom included but embodying his full title — is simple and in harmony with the script, showing self-knowledge and an awareness of his true condition.

Charlotte Brontë (1816-1855) *Opening page of 'Jane Eyre', 1847, plus contemporary signature.*
Literary merit has few links here with principle or philosophy. In spite of the considerable contribution made by the upper case, this is a downward pulled hand with instinct ruling overall:

There are strange and remarkable pressures throughout the writing. Once we have noted the forward slope, reasonably sociable spacing, and light but undiminished *t*-strokes, we leave behind the caring and affectionate mother figure (*M*), and enter a mind tortured by its own inner vitality.

Duty calls strongly in the *b* and *f*, the many rightward pulled understrokes and the retrospective upper loops, but for each one of these there are both repressed and sweeping understrokes, and uneven uprights filled with now flaring, now simmering emotion.

The abundance of inked-in *e*'s indicates secrets firmly enclosed, and the signature a dislike for intimacy. (Her usual preference for 'C. Bell' shows a wish to keep matters on a manageable, business-like footing whilst hiding her sexual identity.)

Fiery impulses spring from below — note the personal *I* leading them upwards into a safely secret knot — and may only be safely expressed in imaginative writing, all other outlets being largely

Jane Eyre
by ~~George Bell~~
~~Lot~~

Currer Bronte

Chap. 1st

There was no possibility of taking a walk that day.
We had been wandering indeed in the leafless shrubbery
an hour in the morning, but since dinner (Mrs Reed,
when there was no company, dined early) the cold winter
wind had brought with it clouds so sombre, a rain so penetrating that further out-door exercise was now out of the
question.
  I was glad of it ; I never liked long-walks — especially
on chilly afternoons ; dreadful to me was the coming home
in the raw twilight with nipped fingers and toes and a heart
saddened by the chidings of Bessie, the nurse, and humbled
by the consciousness of my physical inferiority to Eliza, John
and Georgiana Reed.
  The said Eliza, John and Georgiana were now clustered
round their mamma in the drawing-room ; she lay reclin-

Charlotte Brontë

repressed. The consistent lack of all margins indicates reckless commitment, the open *a*'s and *o*'s an abandoning of discretion, the random *i*-dots diversified interest. Had she been born in a less restricting age, there seems little doubt that Charlotte Brontë's fire would have burned with a more physical vigour, and thus might possibly have been lost to literature.

Johannes Brahms (1833-1897) *Letter headed 1854, signed 1853!* This elegant, controlled writing soars and plunges in a swooping motion, seemingly binding and translating the unworldly into the worldly:

Deep pressure marks the page in rhythmic alternation with fine, light strokes, whilst emotion flows untroubled in the upper loops. Soft and yielding formations blend into the slim, angular script, the merest tremors betraying pain, anxiety or exertion. Such is the writing of an artist beguiled by his own art, a visionary rapt in the expression of his vision.

Skill is added to inspiration in the precise *i* dots and orderly presentation; the script style is unblemished after many such pages. But the *t*-strokes, joined low in obsessional application, betray the untiring effort and supremely high standard of achievement which the composer set for himself. Versatility or innovation is shown by the varying capitals — *G* and *H* especially — but a unity of rhythm blends and transmutes both this and the physical or emotional frustration occasionally found in jarred strokes or stray loops. Encroachment is rarely seen, although the deep spurs of channelled physical strength sometimes merge, in accordance with Brahms' unique pattern, into the newly forming lines of philosophical (upper case) inspiration.

Close word spacing and even uprights suggest a man who relates well to others, but the proud *M* and the differing signature-forms in correspondence show him to be as selective and discriminating in his affections as he is in musical composition.

Johannes Brahms

Appendix A
A Sample Analysis

With the writer's permission, I have chosen this sample of detailed analysis from the many I have been asked to make during recent years. The writer is a school-leaver who has asked for a character study with particular reference to career suitability.

Miss T.

> Dear Mrs Gullan-Whur,
>
> I am writing to you to ask you to analyse my handwriting
>
> I have enclosed pieces which I have written at different times plus all my different signatures as you asked.
>
> P.s I am particularly interested in what sort of career you think I am suited too.

> (1) The Bourbons were to be restored to the French throne — Louis XVIII under a charter which guaranteed parliam"Indemnity + army of occupation
> (2) Prussia was asking for Alsace + Lorraine England + Russia opposed — Prussia gained territories along the Rhine
>   Prussia in dam possit looking after Ger it
> (3) The Czar wanted Poland to become a kingdom under his kingship in compensation Prussia was to be given parts

This writing shows immense frustration in several parts of the writer's life, and I am glad to have the chance of analyzing it, since it may show her what is happening. It is strong writing, and she is quite capable of bringing about her own personal fulfilment.

The flow of the writing is held back with great self-control, and shows initially someone who has had severe blows to her self-esteem in the past. The naturally upright (independent) slope has been pushed backwards, showing that other people are held at arm's length and not allowed to enter certain private thoughts and plans. This contrasts with the affectionate and open nature of the writer, but her fears of being misunderstood, thwarted or ridiculed will not allow her to 'let go'.

The refusal to 'let go' extends into other facets of the personality, and this is best illustrated by a diagram:

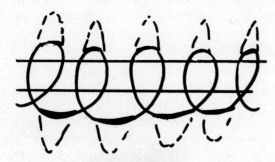

Upper case repressed — could extend higher.

Good middle case.

Lower case repressed — could extend lower.

The writer has the potential to explore imaginatively or philosophically, and is capable of good spiritual understanding. She may be alarmed by this statement, as indeed her shortened upper strokes show that she is alarmed by flights of fancy or anything unlinked to logic, but in fact she is gifted with a balanced personality which could include this type of brain activity.

This writing is also inhibited on the physical level, showing physical frustration. The writer does not always find it easy to express herself in her actions, and again sometimes feels that others try to prevent her from doing what she wants to. The lower *f*'s formation shows angry frustration and is not often found in the writing of young people: it more often occurs in the writing of middle-aged people who feel they are tied to a tread-mill and given no scope to do things their way. Is this how she feels? Other features in the samples such as the loops in *d*'s and *t*'s support this outlook, showing a feeling that no one knows how hard she tries to please, and to achieve. The understroke in the signature shows physical self-consciousness.

The *y* loop tries to stay close to the central, mental case, as though she fears that her form of physical self-expression will be disapproved of by others.

The writer is strong-willed and likes to have her own way, and I must say that her logical thought processes are quite sound enough for her to be ninety per cent sure of her own judgement. The remaining doubtful ten per cent is due to her expectancy of opposition, which may sometimes be imagined. There are signs that she could be a good practical organizer, and attention to detail is normally excellent. If given a job with responsibility and scope for self-expression, I feel that much of the tension and frustration at present in the writing would disappear.

Although the logical thought processes are strong, the writer is also motivated by emotion, and by the correct order of rhythm of events. Because all these three motivations are present in the writing, she may at times have difficulty in making decisions. I will try to make that clearer: the thinking brain is moving ahead with some bright ideas but the feelings are not happy about them. At the same time a slowing and checking impulse insists that things be done according to a set pattern. All this is evident in the history notes, and the result there is one not of frustration, but of harmony. These differing impulses can all be put to work together, but the writer must learn to recognize when they are in opposition to one another, and to face the fact that it is often her own nature that prevents her from going ahead with things, and not other people. It would be helpful to keep constant checks on what each part of her mind — the logical, the emotional, and the practical organizer — is demanding at that moment. This is an affectionate person, but she is independent, fairly self-sufficient, and certainly not always in need of company.

The most recent writing, that is, the letter to me, shows greater relaxation all round, and although the features previously discussed are present, they are not as marked or as intense. The lines of writing are level and the uprights parallel, showing no emotional disturbance. The signature is *slightly* self-projected showing a *slight* fear of being ignored, but more significant is the tightness of the writing of my name, showing some anxiety or distaste. My guess is that this is a combination of fending off the unknown and imaginative quality of graphology, and bracing against yet more adult assessment. Yet the letter is relaxed and as a letter of job application would be impressive.

The writer asks about a suitable career. In her case I think it is more important to know what would be unsuitable, and I do not think she would be happy in any job where she had to change direction quickly at someone else's whim or will. She needs to move at her own pace. She will suffer, too, if not treated quietly and with affection, and this points to a career which is sheltered from the general public. Her warm nature suggests working with children, and her practical capability and liking for order and pattern would support this strongly. She would be happiest if in charge, but would get through the training quite happily if allowed to move at her own speed. I do not think she is suited to an intellectual career, simply because it would not use enough of her personality and gifts, and she would feel stifled and unfulfilled. The things to look for in a career are small numbers of people, freedom to work at her own pace, varied activity including the imaginative and the physical, and a chance to have ultimate responsibility. She would be a good boss because her sense of order, attention to detail and warmth of personality would back up her own instinctive understanding of the horrors of being chivvied.

I need hardly add that the writer has all the qualities needed to be a good housewife and mother, but must choose a husband who will let her move at her own pace.

Appendix B
Some Questions Answered

The following are some of the questions I am frequently asked, but whose answers had no obvious place in the earlier sections of the book.

1. Can you analyze foreign handwriting?

I can analyze anything written in the Roman (our) alphabet. To understand vertical and lateral pressures it is necessary to be familiar with the letter formations.

2. Can you analyze italic writing?

Sometimes. When the writer is adhering to perfect or classical formations he is stylizing his handwriting and deliberately controlling the flow. Characteristics and attributes often do show through, but on the whole such a writer is setting up an aesthetic facade behind which he hides. This attitude is usually a genuine and conscious attempt to beautify his life, but the element of façade may extend to the personality itself.

3. Surely the way you're taught to write influences your writing?

Yes, just as the way you are taught to do anything else influences or fails to influence you. People who form letters in exactly the way they were taught to when they were under ten years old are conformists. Their writing shows that they respect authority and are probably still mentally obeying their parents. Most of us form our own opinions and principles as we grow up, and listen to the inner guidance of our own unique personality. Thus variations creep into our writing.

4. Why do I have more than one style of writing?

Very probably you do not. Your second 'style' may be a slightly disintegrated version of your first, made sloppy by boredom, tiredness or writer's fatigue. Most graphologists would recognize indentical characteristics in the two styles in such a case.

However, some people really do have two distinctive styles, showing two different attitudes. It is possible to isolate the two attitudes by noting on what occasions the two styles are used. Sometimes a situation produces fear, which will tilt the writing backwards. This subject is discussed in Changes and in Conflict.

5. Why do I need to turn the paper sideways in order to write horizontally across the page?

I think you are supporting your elbow or forearm on the table.

6. Does it make any difference how you hold your pen?

This is all part of the writer's character, and tension will show in white knuckles as much as in tightened writing. Physical problems will dictate certain unusual ways of holding the pen, but the amount of manual control will generally remain comparable to brain control.

7. Can you see homosexual tendencies in writing?

No. I can only recognize physical repression, self-consciousness, fastidiousness, anxiety or repression. If these are not present in writing, and I see only a physically fulfilled personality, as far as I am concerned there is no aberration. If the above signs are present they can apply equally to homosexual or heterosexual people, so are no guide.

8. Does that mean you cannot tell the sex of the writer?

It is never possible to do more than guess, and I do not guess sex. So-called masculine and feminine features lie within all our personalities: graphology can only recognize human qualities, tendency and potential.

9. What about age?

Again, graphology is solely concerned with qualities. Signs of absent-mindedness may appear in the young, and physical zest or artlessness in the old. I am prepared to make a guess in police work, going by several tendencies in the writing.

Index

This index includes only those facets of writing which cannot be located directly from the lists of contents and alphabetical formations.